Leaders and Thinkers in American History

A HISTORY BOOK FOR KIDS

LEADERS AND THINKERS
in American History

A HISTORY BOOK FOR KIDS

★ 15 INFLUENTIAL PEOPLE YOU SHOULD KNOW ★

Megan DuVarney Forbes

Illustrations by Amanda Lenz

ROCKRIDGE
PRESS

For general information on our other products and services or to obtain technical support, please contact our Customer Care Department within the United States at (866) 744-2665, or outside the United States at (510) 253-0500.

Rockridge Press publishes its books in a variety of electronic and print formats. Some content that appears in print may not be available in electronic books, and vice versa.

TRADEMARKS: Rockridge Press and the Rockridge Press logo are trademarks or registered trademarks of Callisto Media Inc. and/or its affiliates, in the United States and other countries, and may not be used without written permission. All other trademarks are the property of their respective owners. Rockridge Press is not associated with any product or vendor mentioned in this book.

Series Designer: William Mack
Interior and Cover Designer: John Clifford
Art Producer: Hannah Dickerson
Editor: Laura Bryn Sisson
Production Editor: Sigi Nacson
Production Manager: Martin Worthington

Illustrations © 2021 Amanda Lenz
Author photo courtesy of Yanira Joy
Illustrator photo courtesy of Mai Anh Nguyen

ISBN: Print 978-1-64876-076-1 | eBook 978-1-64876-077-8
R0

To my son, Jenson.
You will make history
one day!

Contents

Introduction

When we face difficult times, and the future is uncertain, it can help to look to the leaders of the past and learn about how they managed, made change, served, and sacrificed for people less fortunate than themselves. This book is meant to empower you to do the same.

George Washington's life illustrates the very first values that American politicians shared. Tecumseh teaches us about the power of being true to yourself and defending your community. Lucretia Mott shows us how to stand up against what is wrong and speak out for what is right. Through Thomas Edison, we can learn to light up the world by dedicating ourselves to problem-solving, despite failure after failure.

There is no single right way to make a difference. When Ida B. Wells saw violence and inequality, she grabbed her pen and paper to research and write about

what was happening. Dorothea Lange documented hardship as well, through photographs that always captured beauty alongside pain.

Daniel Inouye was once viewed as an enemy by his own country, but he sacrificed to protect and advocate for his fellow Americans. Martin Luther King Jr. read about the history of the United States, just as you are doing right now, and demanded that the government live up to its ideals.

These leaders used their own gifts and talents to impact the world around them. Look to them for inspiration. What are your gifts? How can you use them to help others? We are counting on you to be a leader in the future—and maybe even now! In uncertain times, learn from the past, and let history inspire you to make the world a better place.

George
WASHINGTON
(1732–1799)

As the first president of the United States, George Washington shared in the successes and struggles of the new nation. Through his life we can learn about the dreams, frustrations, and challenges of the early United States.

George was born in the British colony of Virginia on February 22, 1732. His parents were Augustine and Mary, and he was the oldest of their six children. The Washingtons owned a lot of land, but they could not afford to send George to boarding school, as many wealthy families did at the time. Instead, he studied with private tutors. He read books, conducted experiments, and learned from his older half brother Lawrence and from his neighbors, the Fairfax family. He studied math and geography, and read about agriculture.

When George was only eleven years old, his father died. George helped his mother raise his younger siblings and manage the plantation where they lived. When he was seventeen, his neighbor helped George get a job as a **land surveyor**. Surveyors explored lands and created maps of where the rivers, mountains, roads, and towns were located.

The land that George surveyed had been inhabited by Indigenous Peoples, who used to be called Native Americans or Indians, for about ten thousand years. In the 1740s, when George traveled through the Shenandoah Valley in Virginia, however, the land was mostly occupied by traders and settlers from France and Germany. His job as a surveyor helped him acquire wealth and property.

In the early 1750s, George was inspired by his half brother Lawrence to join the Virginia militia. He became a soldier at age twenty-one. The British controlled much of the East Coast, from Virginia up to Nova Scotia in Canada, at that time. Meanwhile, the French governed the territory to the west, from Louisiana up to the northern border.

The British sent George to an area west of Virginia, called the Ohio territory. He was instructed to tell the French to leave the land that the British claimed as theirs. This led to a war between the French and the British, which came to be known as the French and Indian War (1754–1763). Indigenous tribes fought on both sides of the war, depending on which side they had formed an alliance with. George gained a lot of military experience during these battles.

In 1759, George married a wealthy widow named Martha Custis, who already had two children. While George was serving in the military, he and Martha exchanged many letters expressing how much they loved each other. Little did Martha know that she would become the original First Lady of the United States.

George and Martha held many people in slavery on their plantation, or large farm, even though George repeatedly said in letters to his wife that he wanted slavery **abolished**. Slavery became a major issue as the young country was being formed.

The French lost the French and Indian War in 1763, and largely left North America. The British began taxing the colonists heavily to pay for their war debts, even though the colonies had no representatives in the British Parliament looking out for their interests.

In 1775, the frustrated colonists created the Continental Army and George Washington was appointed its commander-in-chief. When King George III of England refused to give in to the colonists' demands for representation, a war of independence broke out. For the next six years, the colonists fought in the Revolutionary War, with George as their leader.

> **"LIBERTY, WHEN IT BEGINS TO TAKE ROOT, IS A PLANT OF RAPID GROWTH."**

The British army was one of the most powerful armies in the world. At the beginning of the American Revolution, George and his men lost many battles. But, in one of his most famous victories, George snuck across the Delaware River from Pennsylvania in the middle of the night on Christmas 1776, and attacked the Hessian army on the other side in New Jersey. The Hessians were German fighters the British had hired to help them in the war. The victory marked a turning point in the war for the Continental Army.

In the fall of 1781, George and his troops captured more than seven thousand British soldiers in Yorktown, Virginia, and the British surrendered. The United States was free from British rule!

For six years, the thirteen colonies—now called states—were governed by the **Articles of Confederation**. But each state had different kinds of money, soldiers still hadn't been paid for their service during the Revolutionary War, and there was no way to settle disputes between states.

After the war, George returned to his home in Mount Vernon. But in 1787, the delegates (or representatives) to the Constitutional Convention, begged George to lead their meetings as they tried to put together a new, stronger form of government.

One issue that both the convention and George had to confront was slavery. Nearly half the delegates to the convention were slaveholders, including George himself. Even though he said he was morally opposed to slavery, he still kept his own workers in slavery throughout his lifetime.

George's fellow Virginians also argued about how the issue of slavery would affect the new government. Because so many people were enslaved in the state of Virginia, Virginia's representatives wanted slaves to count toward the state's population. This would give Virginia more representatives in the new Congress. However, **abolitionists** (people who believed slavery should be outlawed) argued that if enslaved workers were counted as people, rather than property, then slaveholders had no right to buy and sell them for labor. In the face of this moral and legal dispute, the members of the convention forged a peculiar compromise. They said that enslaved people would count as three-fifths of a person toward a state's population. Eventually, they agreed upon, or **ratified**, the United States Constitution in 1789.

After the ratification, George Washington was **unanimously** elected by the Electoral College—representatives from each state who officially choose the president—as the president of the United States. Everyone at the convention agreed he was the best choice. In this new role, he was careful to be as fair as possible, and not to act like a king. He chose several men to help him govern, including Thomas Jefferson and Alexander Hamilton. George also chose members of the first Supreme Court, took the first **census** to find out how many people lived in the United States, and imposed taxes to help pay off the nation's debts.

George served as president for eight years, or two four-year terms. He believed the nation and the Constitution were strong enough to last without him, and he stepped down from the presidency in 1796. He wrote a letter, called Washington's Farewell Address, to say goodbye to public service. In it, he urged people to stay united as Americans, to rely on the **checks and balances** in the Constitution, and to be good, moral people.

EXPLORE MORE! Check out the Mount Vernon website (MountVernon.org) to take a virtual tour of Washington's home.

TIPS FOR YOU! Former presidents have really cool libraries with lots to explore, usually located in their hometowns. Find out if there is a presidential library near you.

TECUMSEH
(1768–1813)

The Indigenous Peoples who lived in America in the 1800s were just as diverse and different from one another as the nations and people in Europe. Indigenous tribes spoke different languages from one another, had different governments, wore different clothes, and built different kinds of houses. And they often fought wars against one another. They did have one thing in common, however—their opposition to the settlers from Europe and the American colonies who wanted to take their land. A leader named Tecumseh made it his life's mission to bring these tribes together and see themselves as one people to resist the invading settlers.

Tecumseh was born in 1768. He was a member of the Shawnee people, who inhabited the Ohio River Valley. (In the Shawnee language, his name was Tecumethe, but English speakers pronounced it "Tecumseh.") Tecumseh had several brothers and sisters, and his best friend was Stephen Ruddell, a white boy who grew up with the Shawnee.

When Tecumseh was a child, England still controlled the American colonies. England had made a treaty with Indigenous tribes, promising that colonists would not settle on the land in the Ohio territory, where Tecumseh's family lived. However, many settlers still invaded the Ohio territory, and Tecumseh grew up seeing conflicts between the Shawnee people, the British, the American colonists, the French, and other Indigenous tribes.

Tecumseh trained to be a great warrior, like his father and brothers. He was an accomplished hunter, he was athletic—almost six feet tall—and he had lots of friends. When he was a teenager, Tecumseh was inspired by the alliance between tribes forged by the Shawnee war chief named Blue Jacket. The tribes were very different, yet Blue Jacket was able to bring them together. Tecumseh wanted to be such a leader. He learned to be an outstanding speaker, so that he could meet with the leaders of other tribes and nations, to help prevent future wars.

Many years after the Revolutionary War, in 1810, Tecumseh sat down with the Indiana territorial governor, William Henry Harrison (who would later become the ninth president of the United States). The Americans had recently signed the Treaty of Fort Wayne with several Indigenous tribes, taking more than three million acres of land from these tribes. Tecumseh did not believe that this treaty was legal. His people had not signed the treaty, yet they would be forced to move as well.

> **"NO TRIBE HAS THE RIGHT TO SELL, EVEN TO EACH OTHER, MUCH LESS TO STRANGERS. SELL A COUNTRY?! WHY NOT SELL THE AIR, THE GREAT SEA, AS WELL AS THE EARTH?"**

Tecumseh spoke passionately, and used an interpreter. He wanted to be sure that his message was always clear. At the time, many people spoke several languages in order to trade and communicate with all the different people they might encounter. It was useful to know English, French, and Spanish, as well as Indigenous languages, like Iroquois and Cherokee.

Tecumseh warned Harrison that the Shawnee would make an alliance with the British if the Americans didn't **renegotiate** the treaty. The Americans had won the Revolutionary War against the British about thirty years earlier, but the British still controlled parts of Canada. However, Tecumseh could see that the Americans had no intention of changing the treaty. So, for several years he traveled to dozens of different Indigenous nations, urging them to create one strong alliance that could fight back against the American settlers. Tecumseh convinced many tribes to join his resistance against American settlers on native lands. This became known as Tecumseh's Confederacy.

Meanwhile, Tecumseh's younger brother, Tenskwatawa, was a major influence on him. Tenskwatawa was also known as the Prophet. He saw how many Indigenous People were **assimilating** to a more European way of life, and he thought that this was weakening their own culture. He preached against wearing European-style shirts and trousers, as many Indigenous People did, and warned against the dangers of drinking alcohol. Tecumseh stopped wearing European clothes and went back to wearing deerskin leggings and moccasins. Even in the early 1800s, some Indigenous People thought that Tecumseh and Tenskwatawa were too old-fashioned. Some of them believed that the best way to make peace with Americans and Europeans was to dress like them and adopt some elements of their culture. Nonetheless, many other Indigenous People agreed with the two brothers that they should maintain their own culture and way of life. They formed a village called Prophetstown in Indiana. Over time, the town grew to include thousands of followers.

In 1811, while Tecumseh was traveling through the South recruiting other tribes to join his mission, William Henry Harrison moved a thousand troops into Tecumseh's territory. Tenskwatawa was in Prophetstown and staged an attack on the American troops. But Harrison's forces overpowered them, burned down the town, and destroyed all the food they had put in storage. This was called the Battle of Tippecanoe, and white Americans celebrated Harrison for his victory. Tecumseh and his people, however, were absolutely devastated.

The following year, the Americans and the British officially launched the War of 1812. Hostilities between the British and the French had been brewing for years in Europe. The Americans had little to do with this, except that the Americans' merchant ships were being seized by the British. The Americans also didn't like having the British so close to their northern border. Because Britain and France both still held land in Canada, the tensions crossed the Atlantic.

Tecumseh and his allies sided with the British. They saw this as yet another way to keep the Americans from continuing to move west. Tecumseh and his men won several major battles near the Michigan territory. Ultimately, the war basically ended in a tie. The United States didn't gain any new territory in Canada, and the British would not stop the Americans from moving into Indigenous land. On October 5, 1813, in the Battle of the Thames (in Ontario, Canada), Tecumseh was shot in the chest by an American soldier and died.

Tecumseh died fighting for what he believed in. Many people still imagine America as a land of wide-open space that settlers simply walked into and built upon. Tecumseh's story is just one example of how, for hundreds of years, many Indigenous People fought passionately to keep control of their lands. They made alliances, fought in wars, disagreed with other tribes, and joined together in resistance. To many Americans today, Tecumseh is an example of true heroism and bravery.

EXPLORE MORE! Whenever you are studying a war or a battle in American history, make sure to look up which Indigenous tribes were also engaged in the fighting. Sometimes they are left out of history books, but Indigenous People were involved in every battle in U.S. history.

TIPS FOR YOU! Which Indigenous tribe lived on the land where you are right now? Go to Native-Land.ca and type in the name of your city or town to find out.

Lucretia
MOTT
(1793–1880)

Lucretia Coffin was born on January 3, 1793, on the island of Nantucket in Massachusetts. Like many men on the island, her father was a ship's captain and was away at sea for months at a time. The women on the island stayed behind and ran all the businesses and households. From a young age, Lucretia saw that women were capable of anything they set their minds to. Lucretia's family were Quakers, a religion that believes that all humans are equal and that everyone has a divine light. Unlike most churches at that time, the Quakers, or the Society of Friends, allowed women to be preachers.

Girls received the same education as boys at Quaker schools, which was not very common in America in the early 1800s. Lucretia learned from her teachers that because every human is equal, slavery was wrong. During this time, slavery was common—mostly in the Southern states. Lucretia read about the evils of slavery and learned about people who were fighting to end—or abolish—slavery.

At age fifteen, Lucretia completed her studies at Nine Partners Quaker Boarding School in New York State. She became an assistant teacher there and met a fellow assistant teacher named James Mott. The two shared passionate beliefs about equality and the need to end slavery, and their friendship turned to romance. When Lucretia's family moved to Philadelphia, James came with them. Lucretia married James in 1811 when she was eighteen years old, and the couple had six children. While they were both teachers, one thing Lucretia observed was that her husband made twice the salary of the head teacher, who was a woman. She didn't think this was fair. She always noticed when people were not being treated equally, and she always spoke up.

When Lucretia was twenty-eight years old, she became a minister in the Society of Friends. James had also left teaching to become a cotton merchant. Lucretia was a talented speaker and preached at churches about the importance of abolishing slavery. Lucretia and James hated slavery so much that they refused to buy any products that had been produced by slave labor. They **boycotted** sugar and tobacco, and James even gave up his cotton business because he knew that enslaved people in the South grew and picked the cotton. He started a new business with wool fabrics instead.

The Motts' home in Philadelphia was always full of visitors. Fellow activists—both Black and white—dropped by to talk, eat, and ask for advice. In 1833, Lucretia founded the Philadelphia Female Anti-Slavery Society. Even though women did not have the right to vote, they wrote to their government representatives and asked them to pass laws that would outlaw slavery. However, for eight years, from 1836 to 1844, Congress refused to even bring up the issue of slavery. Lucretia and her fellow activists knew they would need to convince Americans that slavery was wrong.

> **"LET US PUT OUR OWN SOULS IN THEIR SOULS' STEAD, WHO ARE IN SLAVERY, AND LET US LABOR FOR THEIR LIBERATION AS BOUND WITH THEM."**

Lucretia became famous for her passionate speeches about equality for women and for African Americans. In the late 1830s, she attended the national Anti-Slavery Convention of American Women. This annual convention brought together women representatives from many states to discuss their role in the abolition movement. And in 1840, she traveled to London to attend the World's Anti-Slavery Convention. Lucretia was one of just six women delegates.

Many religious people did not think that Lucretia had the right to preach in rooms with men and women, and to tell men what to do. Once she got sick while she was traveling and a doctor refused to treat her because he didn't like her sermons.

Lucretia met other famous activists, including Elizabeth Cady Stanton and Susan B. Anthony, who were well-known advocates for women's **suffrage**. In 1848, Lucretia joined with Elizabeth to organize the Seneca Falls Convention. This two-day meeting was the first women's rights convention in the United States. All three women believed in the abolition of slavery and in women's right to vote. Lucretia's unwavering belief in equality meant that she could not separate her devotion to women's rights from her devotion to African Americans' rights. She wrote that she was committed to "human rights" above all else.

Together with two very famous abolitionists, William Lloyd Garrison and Frederick Douglass, Lucretia spoke out against Christians who used the Bible to defend slavery. William was a white journalist who used his newspaper, *The Liberator*, to argue that slavery needed to be abolished. Frederick, who had been enslaved but was now free, wrote and spoke about the horrible conditions endured by enslaved people. Lucretia believed that slavery was not only cruel to enslaved people but also that it was bad for the slaveholders because it made them wicked and inhumane.

During the Civil War years (1861–1865), Lucretia, like all Quakers, did not support the war. She was a **pacifist**. However, she was glad when the North won and the Thirteenth Amendment, outlawing slavery, was adopted.

Lucretia became a member of the Joint Committee on Indian Affairs. This group of Quakers was formed to help the Seneca tribe fight for their rights to their land in New York State. At the end of her life she regretted that she had not done more to get to know members of Indigenous tribes and to advocate for their land rights.

When Lucretia was in her seventies, she joined the Friends Association for the Aid and Elevation of the Freedmen. This Quaker organization supported African Americans who were starting a new life. She spoke at Black churches in the city of Philadelphia, and she volunteered at a home for elderly African Americans. Years later, when she was eighty, Lucretia arranged to meet with President Ulysses S. Grant. She successfully advocated for the lives of a group of Indigenous Modoc men who had been involved in an uprising in Northern California. As she had always done, she used her voice and her influence to fight against injustice.

Lucretia Mott lived to the age of eighty-seven. When she died in 1880, women still did not have the right to vote. But she had spent her entire life fighting to make sure that women—and people of all races—were treated equally and were given the respect they deserved.

EXPLORE MORE! Lucretia Mott made sure that she was not buying goods made by slave labor. Today we can buy products labeled "Fair Trade" to make sure that we are doing the same thing. Look for fair trade products the next time you go to a store.

TIPS FOR YOU! Lucretia was a member of dozens of clubs and organizations! Join a club at your school to learn something cool and make new friends.

Ulysses S. GRANT

(1822–1885)

A Civil War general on the side of the Union and the eighteenth president of the United States, Ulysses S. Grant was born on April 27, 1822, in Ohio. His parents named him Hiram Ulysses Grant, but he usually went by Ulysses, the name of a famous Greek hero. He loved horses and he was quiet, like his mother. Ulysses attended Maysville Seminary School in Kentucky.

In 1839, Ulysses's father asked a congressman to write a letter of recommendation to get his son into the best military academy in the United States, West Point. The congressman thought that Ulysses's name was Ulysses S. Grant (maybe because his mother's maiden name was Simpson), so that's what he wrote in the letter. This name was entered into the official file at West Point, and Ulysses was stuck with it for the rest of his life. Years later, when his wife asked him what his middle initial stood for, he said, "I don't know!"

At West Point, Ulysses learned math, geography, engineering, and history, in addition to **military strategy**.

When he graduated in 1843, he didn't think he wanted to stay in the military as a career. But he had to fulfill his required military service. In 1846, he was sent to Mexico to fight in the Mexican-American War. Tensions had arisen between the two countries after the United States annexed (that is, took over) Texas, eventually leading to war. During the war, Ulysses saw that the United States was trying to gain more territory to create more states where slavery could be legal. Ulysses believed that slavery was wrong.

Ulysses was engaged to Julia Dent for four years while he was away fighting. Ulysses and Julia loved each other very much. Julia's parents held people in slavery, however, and Ulysses's parents believed that slavery was wrong, so there was always tension between the two families. The couple married in 1848 and had four children.

In 1860, Abraham Lincoln was elected president. During the election, Lincoln's platform (the things politicians say they will do if they are elected) had opposed expanding slavery into the Western territories. Seven states in the South predicted that Lincoln would make slavery illegal. Their economies relied heavily on slave labor. So they left the United States and formed their own country. They called their country the Confederate States of America, also known as the Confederacy. The states in the North became known as the Union. The Union now had twenty states, and the Confederacy expanded to include eleven states. In April 1861,

Confederate forces attacked Fort Sumter in South Carolina, and the Civil War officially began.

Ulysses joined the Union army in 1861. At first, the army didn't give Ulysses an official position, but in September he was appointed to command troops in Illinois. He applied the skills he had learned during the Mexican-American War to his battle strategies against the Confederate troops. When he won the first major victory for the Union in the Battle of Fort Donelson in 1862, he earned the nickname "Unconditional Surrender Grant" (playing off his initials, "U.S."). Ulysses allowed the Confederate troops to keep their belongings when they surrendered, and he gave them food and medical care. Because so many troops died on both sides during Grant's battles, he never allowed his soldiers to cheer after a victory.

From 1862 to 1864, Grant won decisive victories against the Confederacy and became the leader of the Union army. He got along well with his soldiers and kept them motivated through brutal conditions. By 1863, African Americans were fighting on the side of the Union, and the North was winning battles in Vicksburg and Chattanooga.

On April 9, 1865, the Confederate troops were outnumbered and surrounded near the village of Appomattox Court House in Virginia. Confederate General Robert E. Lee met with General Ulysses S. Grant to discuss terms of surrender. Technically, the Confederate troops could have been considered traitors to the United States, but they were given a pardon and allowed to keep all their belongings, except for any enslaved people. The Union army band started to play a song in celebration of winning the Civil War, but Grant stopped them and said, "The war is over. The Rebels are our countrymen again."

> ## "I HAVE NEVER ADVOCATED WAR EXCEPT AS A MEANS OF PEACE."

The Civil War was the most deadly war in American history. In total, more than 600,000 people died in the war, including soldiers and **civilians** on both sides. After the war, and with the earlier passage of the Emancipation Proclamation, which took effect in 1863, four million enslaved people were freed. The United States remained unified, and the eleven states that had **seceded** were once again part of the country.

Five days after the Confederate army surrendered, President Lincoln was assassinated by John Wilkes Booth in a failed attempt to save the Confederacy. Vice President Andrew Johnson became the president. Andrew Johnson was later **impeached** by Congress, in February 1868. Later that year, Ulysses S. Grant was elected president. Ulysses was forty-six, the youngest president of the United States at that time.

Ulysses worked to reunite the Northern and Southern states after the war. He also protected newly freed

African Americans during this period, known as
Reconstruction. New amendments were added to the
Constitution: the Thirteenth Amendment (1865), which
outlawed slavery; the Fourteenth Amendment (1868),
which guaranteed equal protection to all under the law;
and the Fifteenth Amendment (1869), which gave Black
men the right to vote.

Not all Americans were in favor of these changes,
however. In 1865, several former Confederate soldiers
in Tennessee started a group called the Ku Klux Klan,
or KKK. KKK members terrorized and murdered Black
people. The KKK soon grew to half a million members in
the South.

Ulysses created the U.S. Department of Justice in
1870 to protect African Americans from violence in
the South. He also appointed many Black, Jewish, and
Indigenous men to federal jobs in his administration.
Ely S. Parker was his commissioner for Indian Affairs,
the first Seneca person to hold such a position in the
American government.

Ulysses served two terms as president. Toward the
end of his life, the legendary author Mark Twain encouraged Ulysses to write his **memoirs**. Ulysses was facing
financial ruin when Twain stepped in to help. Grant
died of throat cancer in 1885, three days after finishing
his memoirs.

Ulysses is remembered as one of the greatest generals
in U.S. history. Perhaps even more important, he used his
power as president to defend all American citizens. He is

considered the first civil rights president, overseeing the ratification of some of the most important amendments to the Constitution.

EXPLORE MORE! Explore maps of how Civil War battles and troop movements played out at PBS.org /kenburns/civil-war/war/maps. Maps are a great way to understand military strategy and decisions made during war.

TIPS FOR YOU! The Fourteenth Amendment is really important, because it ensures equal protection for all under the law. As you learn about Supreme Court cases in school, pay attention to how many involve the Fourteenth Amendment.

Harriet
TUBMAN
(1822–1913)

Harriet Tubman, one of the most recognized heroes in civil rights history, was a freedom seeker, activist, and Civil War spy. Throughout her life, she was committed to improving the lives of both African Americans and women.

Harriet was born in 1822 to parents who were enslaved on a plantation in Maryland. Her parents, Harriet and Benjamin, named her Araminta, but called her "Minty" for short. When she was only five years old, Minty had to help raise her younger siblings. The people who enslaved her would also rent her out to neighboring farms.

Minty had to work even if she was sick or injured. One day she received an injury that would affect her for the rest of her life. When she was sent into town to get some supplies, she saw an enslaved man running from an **overseer**. Overseers worked on plantations to make sure that enslaved people followed their unfair rules. This overseer was trying to capture the man, and he asked Minty to help him. When she refused, the overseer threw a weight at her that hit her in the head, cracking her skull. For the rest of her life, Minty suffered from headaches and seizures, making her pass out unexpectedly. She said, however, that when she had these seizures, she also saw visions of freedom.

Minty lived and worked near most of her family members, which was not always the case for enslaved people. Then some of her older sisters were sold to plantations farther south, and Minty's family was torn apart. Minty's sisters even had to leave behind their children. Minty never forgot the pain of losing her sisters.

In her early twenties, Minty met a man named John Tubman, who was a free Black man. When she married John, she took her mother's first name, Harriet, and John's last name. She would be known as Harriet Tubman from then on. Marrying John still did not make Harriet a free woman, however. In those days, such "blended" marriages were common, with free people of color married to enslaved people.

In 1849, Harriet's owner, Edward Brodess, planned to sell Harriet and her family members. Harriet and two of her brothers decided to try to reach freedom in the North before they were sold. Eliza Brodess, Edward's wife, put an advertisement in the newspaper, offering a $300 reward if someone found the three runaways and returned them. The punishment for enslaved people who were caught was very harsh. Harriet's brothers decided to go back and turn themselves in, but Harriet pressed on until she reached Philadelphia, Pennsylvania.

In Philadelphia she found a thriving community of Black people, running businesses and building communities. Many of them had escaped to the North with the help of a network of antislavery activists called the **Underground Railroad**. The "conductors" would use secret messages and codes to let runaways know that their home or barn was a safe place to hide. After the passage of a law called the **Fugitive Slave Law** in 1850, it became legal to kidnap any formerly enslaved person who had escaped to the North and drag them back into slavery in the South. This controversial law made tensions worse between the North and the South.

> **"I HAVE SEEN HUNDREDS OF ESCAPED SLAVES, BUT I NEVER SAW ONE WHO WAS WILLING TO GO BACK AND BE A SLAVE."**

Harriet worked as a cook in Philadelphia. Her husband, John, did not want to come with her, and he eventually married someone else.

Meanwhile, Harriet started planning ways to rescue her family members. When she heard that her niece Kessiah and Kessiah's two children were coming up for auction, Harriet traveled to Baltimore, Maryland, to try to free them. Harriet helped smuggle Kessiah, with her husband and children, to Philadelphia. After losing her older sisters when she was younger, Harriet was determined to do everything she could to reunite her family. In less than two years she returned for six more family members.

Harriet made more than a dozen trips back to Maryland to help people escape. She always moved at night to avoid slave catchers, using the stars as her "map." During the day, they hid in safe houses along the Underground Railroad. There was a $12,000 reward for turning her in, so she had to be very careful. She knew the land well, and she knew how to hide and move quickly. She managed to get all her family members out of Maryland except for three people. This was an amazing accomplishment, but there were still four million people enslaved in the United States.

Throughout the 1850s, Harriet teamed up with other antislavery activists, including Frederick Douglass. Frederick had been enslaved in the past, but was now a well-known author and public speaker. They both gave speeches and told people what it was like to live in bondage. Harriet was also friends with a white senator named William Seward, who worked to end slavery. He helped Harriet purchase a home and a farm in upstate New York, where she could take in people who had escaped from slavery and needed a place to stay.

Because of the work of activists like Harriet and Frederick, many people in the North did not believe that slavery should be legal. But slavery remained part of the economy and culture in the South. So much so, that the Southern states decided to break away and form their own country. They called themselves the Confederate

States of America. In 1861, Confederate troops attacked Fort Sumter in South Carolina, beginning the Civil War.

When the war broke out, Harriet worked as a nurse, helping the injured in South Carolina. Because of her background, she was uniquely qualified to support the North as a spy and a mission commander. In 1863, she led troops down the Combahee River in South Carolina. Just as she had done on her missions rescuing enslaved people, she knew how to move undetected, and she had allies helping her along the way. She and her troops attacked by steamboat along twenty-five miles of the Comba-hee River and burned down plantations and fields. The enslaved people from the plantations ran to the river, chased by Confederate troops, and climbed aboard the steamboats. Harriet and her men were able to rescue more than 750 enslaved people on this single mission! This was the first military campaign in American history to be planned and executed by a woman.

After the North won the Civil War in 1865, Harriet continued to champion the rights of Black people. She returned to upstate New York, where she married a war veteran named Nelson Davis. The couple adopted a girl named Gertie.

Harriet Tubman died in 1913 around the age of ninety-two. She earned the nickname "Moses," after the prophet in the Bible who led the Israelites out of slavery under the Egyptians. She is the only Black woman to have a navy cargo ship, or Liberty ship, named after her—the SS *Harriet Tubman*.

EXPLORE MORE! If you're ever in Cincinnati, Ohio, check out the National Underground Railroad Freedom Center. There, you will learn more about how enslaved people and abolitionists worked together along the Underground Railroad. If you can't make it in person, go to FreedomCenter.org/learn/online-learning -resources/online-exhibits to see their online exhibits.

TIPS FOR YOU! One of Harriet's final projects in her life was to establish a home where she could take care of older people who didn't have other family. Find out if there are any similar facilities in your town with volunteer programs. They often welcome friendly students to come play games and talk with residents!

Thomas
EDISON
(1847–1931)

If you are reading this book in a room with a lightbulb, you are using one of Thomas Edison's inventions. In his lifetime, Thomas Edison patented 1,093 inventions—that averages at least one for every month of his adult life.

Thomas Alva Edison was born on February 11, 1847, in Milan, Ohio. He was the youngest of seven children, and all his siblings had moved out by the time he was a child. His friends in the neighborhood called him "Al." He was able to concentrate so hard and for so long that his teachers at school didn't know how to get him to follow directions and participate. His mother decided to home-school him, and he read every book he could get his hands on. He built himself a laboratory in their basement with more than two hundred bottles of chemicals and potions. He labeled them all POISON so no one would touch them.

Thomas was curious about everything around him. He sat on a neighbor's goose egg for hours to see if he could make it hatch. He burned down his father's barn just to see what it would look like. (His father was not happy.)

When he was twelve, he started selling newspapers on the train for passengers to read. He became fascinated with the telegraph messages that people at the train station sent and received. Around this time, he also started to lose his hearing. Historians don't know why this happened, but later in life he said that he hadn't heard a bird sing since he was twelve years old.

When he was fifteen, Thomas became a telegraph operator. He studied **Morse code**—a series of dots and dashes that represented different letters—for eighteen hours a day and became the fastest telegraph operator in his office. He started inventing different machines that could help transcribe, or spell out, messages quickly. On the side, he also liked to practice forging famous signatures. He could do perfect imitations of George Washington's, Thomas Jefferson's, and Napoleon's handwriting.

In his early twenties, Thomas continued to work for telegraph companies by day. But the inventions he created at night were also becoming quite popular. In 1869, he patented his first invention, an electric vote counter. The machine was designed to record the votes of politicians who were deciding "yes" or "no" on legislation. (They didn't like it.) He also invented the Universal Stock Ticker, which printed constantly updated stock prices on a ticker tape. When he was twenty-three, the Gold & Stock Telegraph Company of New York hired him as a full-time inventor to improve their technology.

On a stormy day in 1871, three schoolgirls took shelter from the rain in the hallway of the building where Thomas worked. He met fifteen-year-old Mary Stilwell and fell in love with her. They got married on Christmas Day when she was sixteen and he was twenty-four. They had three children, although Thomas didn't spend much time with them. He worked all the time and only came home for a few hours a day to sleep. He did give two of his children the nicknames "Dot" and "Dash," the two symbols used in Morse code.

By 1876, Thomas had made enough money from his inventions to build his own laboratory, where he could be a full-time inventor. He built his lab in Menlo Park, New Jersey, and it filled two city blocks. Because he came up with dozens of ideas for inventions every day, he hired a team of engineers who could help him do experiments and test out all his ideas.

During the 1870s, major technological innovations were pioneered, especially when it came to communication and sound. Alexander Graham Bell, Thomas's rival, patented the telephone in 1876. Thomas did not want to be outdone. He wanted to find a way to write down the messages that came through the telephone lines. He started speaking into a cone that would make a tiny pen vibrate onto a piece of tinfoil. When another tiny pen traced over the indentations, the sound came back out through the cone! Thomas Edison had created the first phonograph, a device that could record sound. Reporters came to Menlo

Park from all over to see this device, because people didn't believe that it could be real! He would do demonstrations for reporters, singing "Mary Had a Little Lamb" into the phonograph and then replaying it, to their astonishment.

Thomas wanted to find a way to create a light that would not need a flame or oil. People used oil lamps in their homes already, but these were very dirty and could be dangerous. Thomas and his team worked day and night to create a glass bulb with a filament inside that would give off light for hours at a time. The tiny wire filament inside was the most difficult part to get right.

> **"I HAVE NOT FAILED. I'VE JUST FOUND 10,000 WAYS THAT WON'T WORK."**

On New Year's Eve 1879, trains full of visitors traveled to Menlo Park to witness the great unveiling of Thomas Edison's latest success—the electric lightbulb. They were amazed to see twenty bright lampposts along the walkway and light streaming out of every window. It was like an amusement park for electricity.

For the next few years, Thomas and his large team worked to create an electrical grid (a system of wires through which electricity passes) in Manhattan, New York, to illuminate a whole city block. They had to dig up the streets to install copper wiring and create an entire system to provide electricity to every room in every building. In 1882, Thomas Edison's company created the first power plant in the United States to light up the buildings and the streets. His technology spread all over the world and, very quickly, cities everywhere were freed from the darkness of night.

By this time, Thomas was a millionaire, in addition to being world famous. Sadly, his wife, Mary, died in 1884. He moved out of his laboratory in Menlo Park and created a new laboratory that was ten times larger in West Orange, New Jersey. He married a young woman named Mina in 1886, and they also had three children. He proposed to Mina by tapping Morse code into the palm of her hand.

Thomas continued inventing, even when some of his inventions cost him millions of dollars and weren't successful. But his successes included the machinery inside movie cameras that kept the film moving quickly and evenly. He also made the very first cat video in history, in 1894. People paid five cents to look into a machine called a Kinetoscope and watch a short video of cats boxing!

From Thomas's birth in 1847 to his death in 1931, the world had changed completely. He helped illuminate it with electricity and to connect people through recorded sound and moving pictures. When he died, people turned off their lights all at once for sixty seconds to remember how different their lives were before Thomas Edison gave them electric light.

EXPLORE MORE! We are in the middle of another communications technology boom, like the one Thomas Edison experienced. Make a list of all of the things that didn't exist in the year you were born but that exist today. Then make a list of some inventions you hope will exist soon. Maybe you will invent them!

TIPS FOR YOU! Create your own mini–Menlo Park. Ask your parents to help you look up videos or websites with directions for experiments involving electrical circuits. There are so many that you can do from your house with just a few supplies!

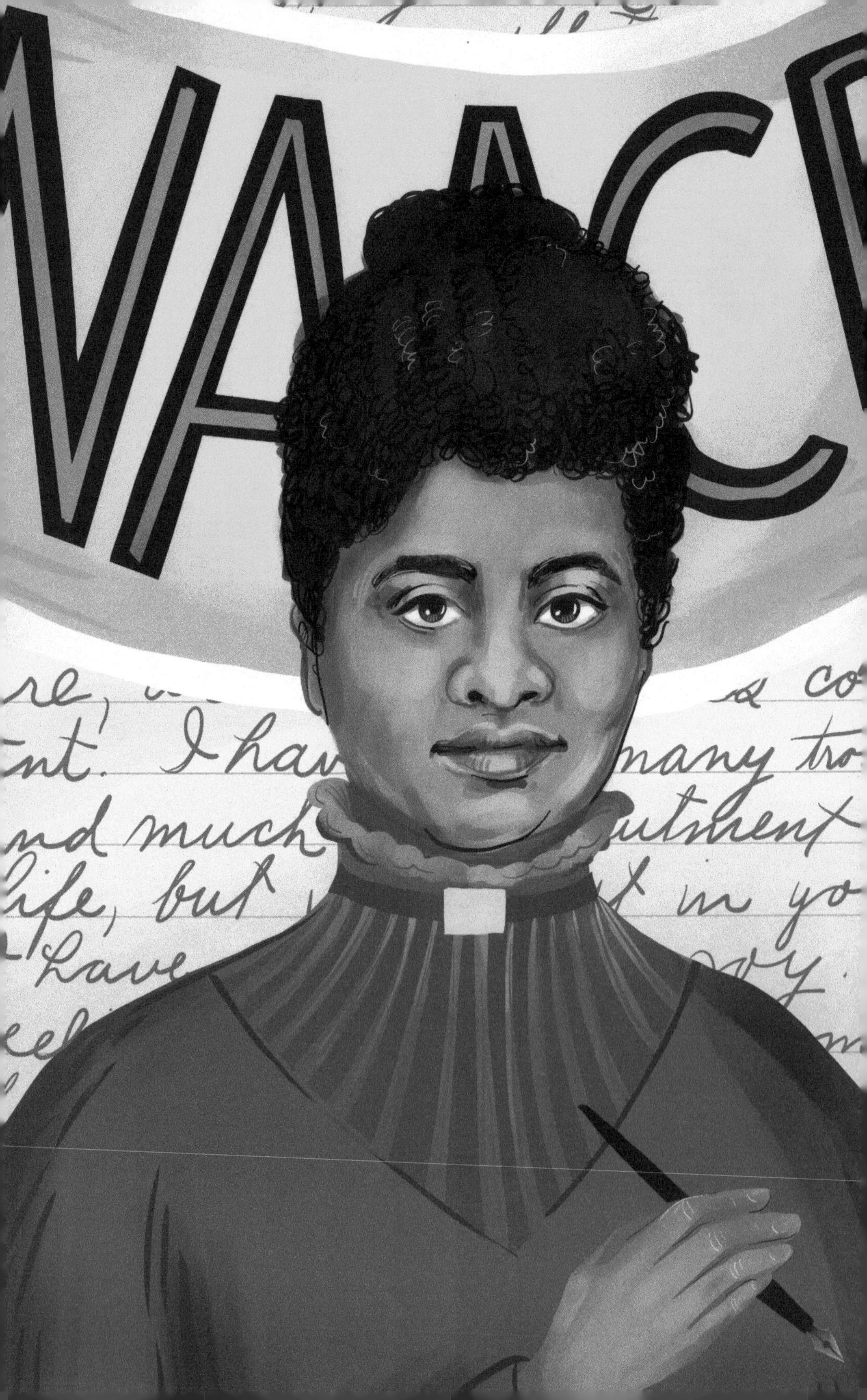

Ida B. WELLS
(1862–1931)

I da B. Wells was a journalist, abolitionist, and feminist. She wrote articles that exposed racial injustices. After women won the right to vote, she worked hard to encourage women, especially Black women, to take part in the voting process and to participate in politics.

Ida was born into slavery in Holly Springs, Mississippi, during America's Civil War (1861–1865), the same year that the Emancipation Proclamation was signed by President Abraham Lincoln. She was the oldest of eight children. After the war, Ida's father was a successful carpenter and later served on the first board of trustees for Rust College in Mississippi.

When Ida was sixteen, both of her parents and a brother died from a terrible disease called yellow fever. Ida, who was then attending Rust College, got a job as a teacher, so she could support her younger brothers and sisters. She and her siblings later moved to Tennessee.

In 1883, Ida bought a first-class train ticket for a section called the Ladies' Car. The train conductor, however, told her that she would have to leave her seat and go sit in the rear car, where Black people rode. Ida said that she had paid for her ticket and would not move. The conductor grabbed her by the arms and ripped off the sleeve of her dress. Ida fought back, scratching the conductor and biting his hand. Two other passengers helped pry Ida out of her seat and throw her off the train. Ida was furious and sued the railroad company! At first, she won her case in the courts, but then the Tennessee Supreme Court upheld the railroad's rule to treat Black passengers unfairly.

Following the Civil War, states in the South began passing **Jim Crow laws**. These laws were meant to separate Black people from white people, and to limit Black people's ability to succeed economically or politically. The term "Jim Crow" comes from a character that a white actor played, making fun of Black people. This time period, with laws specifically designed to discriminate against Black Americans, is thought of by historians as the low point of race relations in the United States.

Despite the discriminatory laws, many Black people in the South were determined to build up their communities and create opportunities for themselves. Under slavery, Black people were not allowed to learn to read or write, so literacy now became important. While she was still teaching, Ida began to write articles about politics and the treatment of Black people for several newspapers, such as the *Memphis Free Speech*. She eventually became co-owner of the newspaper.

Ida had a friend in Memphis, named Thomas Moss, who owned a grocery store called People's Grocery. In his neighborhood, there had been extreme racial tension, and on one early March evening in 1892, a group of police officers and white volunteers arrested Moss and several other Black men they unfairly suspected of planning some kind of attack on the white town residents. On March 9, seventy-five white men surrounded the jail and dragged Moss and two of his Black employees out of the building. They beat the men and then shot them to death.

> **"THE WAY TO RIGHT WRONGS IS TO TURN THE LIGHT OF TRUTH UPON THEM."**

Ida was horrified. As a journalist, she wanted to expose the violence that was happening to Black people in the South. She interviewed eyewitnesses and family members of other victims and researched the history of what is known as **lynching**, putting people to death illegally (usually by hanging). After the Civil War, white mobs and groups like the Ku Klux Klan (see page 29) exploited Jim Crow laws to murder and terrorize Black people without any consequences. Ida's research showed that at least 728 people had been lynched in the South between 1882 and 1891. In 1892, she published a landmark book about lynching called *Southern Horrors*.

Because of what Ida wrote about the horrors of lynching, a white mob stormed her newspaper office and destroyed it. Luckily, she was not there at the time, but she decided that it was not safe for her to live in the South any longer. She moved to Chicago, where she married a fellow activist named Ferdinand Barnett. They had four children. Although there were no Jim Crow laws in Chicago, Black people still faced unfair conditions there. Ida continued to speak out to try to change discriminatory laws and policies.

Ida helped found several organizations dedicated to uplifting Black people, including what would become the National Association for the Advancement of Colored People, or the NAACP. To achieve real equality and influence, she knew she needed to be able to vote. In 1913, women were still not allowed to vote, so she started an organization for Black women to fight for their right to vote, called the Alpha Suffrage Club. She had two white friends, Belle Squire and Virginia Brooks, who also helped her start this organization.

On March 3, 1913, women from around the country flooded the streets of Washington, DC, for a huge parade, called the Woman Suffrage Procession. Eight thousand people came together to show the newly elected president, Woodrow Wilson, that they believed in voting rights for all Americans, regardless of gender. Some white women, however, thought that they could make a stronger case for women's suffrage (voting rights) if white women were the face of the parade and the movement. They wanted all the Black women to march in the back.

Ida, who had been fighting for women's suffrage for years in Chicago, was outraged. So were her friends Belle and Virginia. Some of the organizers explained that they had to do everything they could to get women from the South to support their cause. But Ida responded, "Our women should be as firm in standing up for their principles as the Southern women are for their prejudices." Ida marched in the front of the parade, arm in arm with Belle and Virginia, even as hundreds of Black women were forced to remain at the back of the parade. Seven years later, in 1920, the Nineteenth Amendment was finally passed, granting women the constitutional right to vote. The amendment was the result of nearly a century of work by both white women and many women of color, including Ida B. Wells.

Ida traveled internationally, speaking to audiences about the horrors of lynching in America. She stood up for the rights of all men and women, even when that put her own life in danger. In 1930, Ida ran for State Senate in Illinois. She also wrote an **autobiography** of her journey, called *Crusade for Justice*, but she died in 1931 before she could publish it. (Her daughter Alfreda continued the work and published it for her in 1970.)

EXPLORE MORE! Ida B. Wells ran for State Senate in Illinois. Ask an adult to help you research who represents you in your state's Senate and Assembly, and in the U.S. Senate and House of Representatives. What are their platforms? What do they want to accomplish in government?

TIPS FOR YOU! Writing is a great way to share your opinions and make change, as Ida B. Wells showed. Does your school have a student newspaper? See if you can get involved. Or write a letter to the editor of your local newspaper about something you care about.

Dorothea
LANGE
(1895–1965)

Today many of us can take pictures of anything we see with our phones, but when Dorothea Lange was born on May 26, 1895, very few people had their own cameras. Dorothea grew up in Hoboken, New Jersey. When she was seven years old, she developed a disease called **polio**, and it left her with a permanently twisted foot. This affected her for the rest of her life, but she never let it slow her down.

When Dorothea was a teenager, her parents divorced, and she and her little brother moved to New York City with their mother. Dorothea loved to explore the **architecture** and museums in the city, instead of doing her homework. She graduated from high school in 1912 and briefly went to college to become a teacher. She dropped out because she already knew what she wanted to do with her life—she wanted to be a photographer.

Dorothea volunteered to be an assistant to several successful photographers, and she learned the skills of both photography and business. She wanted to see more of

57

the world, so she and a friend traveled all the way to San Francisco, California. Dorothea took the skills she had learned in New York and opened up an elegant photography studio. By 1921, when she was only twenty-six years old, she was taking portraits for the wealthiest families in San Francisco.

In the 1930s, the United States experienced the **Great Depression**. Millions of Americans lost their jobs, and the country's economy became very unstable. Many people could hardly afford to eat, let alone pay for glamorous portraits, so Dorothea did not have much work. In 1933, the newly elected president, Franklin D. Roosevelt, started lots of government programs to try to provide Americans with jobs. He called this the **New Deal**. There were job openings for photographers to document the conditions around the country, and Dorothea was hired for one of those jobs.

Dorothea was used to taking portraits of very rich people, but now she used her skills to take beautiful pictures of some of the poorest people in America. She took photos of farmworkers in central California. In the mid-1800s, many men had come to California from China during the Gold Rush. Many of these workers later turned to farmwork. After that, workers from Japan, India, the Philippines, and Mexico were also recruited for these jobs. In the 1930s, a lot of white people from the Southern states also migrated to the West because there was more work in California, even though jobs were still very scarce. Dorothea captured images of this very diverse group of men and women working in the California fields.

At the same time, a researcher named Paul Taylor was studying Mexican immigration to the United States. When he saw Dorothea's images, documenting the struggles of the farmworkers, he asked her to join his project. Paul would often interview people while Dorothea took their photos. As the two worked closely together, they fell in love. They both had children from other marriages, but they formed a new family and stayed married for the next thirty years.

As the country struggled to get back on its feet following the Great Depression, a series of severe drought years brought devastation to the Midwest. In states like Oklahoma, Kansas, and Texas, farmers had pulled up most of the natural prairie grasses and exhausted all the topsoil with different crops. A drought followed that caused severe dust storms, and millions of farmers could not grow the crops that they relied upon. Dorothea and Paul were hired to travel through these Midwestern and Southern states to document the conditions people were facing.

While Paul and Dorothea learned the stories of the workers, they lived in the same tough conditions. It was very hot and dusty, and there were flies, fleas, and bad smells. Dorothea wanted Americans to see why government help was necessary, and to see past their prejudices and respect these workers as human beings. Her photos showed the terrible conditions, but they also showed the beauty of people's faces and the love among families. When people saw the powerful images, they could connect to the men, women, and children who were struggling during the Great Depression.

Dorothea Lange's most famous photograph, and the photograph that came to symbolize the Great Depression, is called *Migrant Mother*. In 1936, Dorothea was driving through a small central California town near San Luis Obispo, where people grew peas. She met a woman with a beautiful and tired face who was looking for work while also caring for her six children. She was a waitress by night and tried to get work in the fields by day. Dorothea took a striking photo of her looking off into the distance as she's trying to figure out how they will survive another day. Two of her children rest their heads on her shoulders. The *San Francisco News* published the photo, and, in response, people donated $200,000 to help farmworkers.

> **"THE CAMERA IS AN INSTRUMENT THAT TEACHES PEOPLE HOW TO SEE WITHOUT A CAMERA."**

In 1942, Dorothea got a new assignment in Manzanar, California. On December 7, 1941, the Japanese military had attacked the U.S. naval base in Pearl Harbor, Hawaii.

The United States officially entered World War II, and President Roosevelt ordered all Japanese Americans, many of whom had never been to Japan, taken to camps. These were called **internment camps**, and they were like prisons. Dorothea photographed Japanese American families in their best clothes, waiting patiently in line to get on buses that would take them to camps with shacks for houses. From her photographs taken in the camps, it is clear that Dorothea was outraged that the American government was imprisoning its own citizens. Her photographs highlighted the work ethic, family values, and respectability of the Japanese American families. At the time, the U.S. government censored, or did not allow, anyone to publish Dorothea's eight hundred photographs of the camps. Today, the images are available in the National Archives.

Until her death in 1965, Dorothea Lange continued to take beautiful photos of people who were often overlooked. When her husband, Paul, became a diplomat, she traveled with him to Korea, Vietnam, Egypt, Palestine, and Ecuador, taking pictures of working people and families.

Her famous photos give us a glimpse into what life was like in the United States for the people most affected by the Great Depression and, later, World War II. She shows us that beauty can be found in unexpected places and reminds us who our fellow Americans really are.

EXPLORE MORE! Look up photographs by Dorothea Lange, like *Migrant Mother*. As you look at the people's faces and surroundings, what do you imagine that they were thinking when they were photographed?

TIPS FOR YOU! Walk around your neighborhood and look for something that is beautiful but unnoticed. Take a picture with a cell phone or a camera, and experiment with ways to capture the image from different angles or with different lighting.

Louis

ARMSTRONG

(1901–1971)

If you were born in the 1920s or '30s, and you liked music, you probably would've wanted to take up the trumpet and play like Louis Armstrong. People usually think of Louis as a happy, lovable person who liked to have fun when he played. But when you dig deeper, you'll see that his influence on music—particularly jazz—completely changed the way popular music is performed.

Louis was born on August 4, 1901, in the lively, bustling city of New Orleans, Louisiana. His mother was very young, just sixteen, when she had Louis. And his father left the family shortly afterward. So Louis and his little sister were raised by their grandmother during their early years. By the time Louis was in elementary school he was already doing odd jobs to help bring in money, like selling newspapers. In time, he saved up five dollars to buy himself a cornet (a small trumpet), and it was his most prized possession.

On New Year's Eve in 1912, when Louis was eleven, he shot his stepfather's gun into the air to make a loud sound and celebrate. This got him into big trouble with the police, and his punishment was being sent to a reform school. But at this school they had a marching band, and he practiced his horn-playing. He learned to play classic New Orleans songs on his cornet—songs like "When the Saints Go Marching In." He fell in love with music at that school and never stopped playing for the rest of his life.

Louis's family was poor. After his term at the reform school ended, when Louis was fourteen, he had to start working full time to help earn money for food. As a teenager, he shoveled coal during the day and then played music in bars until four in the morning! At this time, jazz music was just beginning to develop in places like New Orleans, and Louis was learning all the new songs and techniques. He got a job playing music on a Mississippi riverboat, and everyone loved the way he made his cornet sing.

In 1922, Louis moved to Chicago, Illinois, to play with a group called the Creole Jazz Band. Many African Americans were leaving the South for Northern cities at that time. Between 1910 and 1930, the Black population in Chicago grew from 44,000 to 233,000. Louis learned to make records there. Recording jazz music onto vinyl records was a new process, and musicians were still trying to figure out how to get the best sound quality. Louis played so loudly that he had to stand way over in a corner so he didn't drown out all the other instruments!

Louis moved to New York City in 1924, during the height of the **Harlem Renaissance**. As African Americans came to New York in large numbers and lived in mostly Black neighborhoods, they created art and culture that reflected their life experiences. Louis Armstrong and other musicians, like Duke Ellington and Bessie Smith, sold records all over the country. Yet, when Louis and his band traveled for their concerts, they were often not allowed to eat at the restaurants where they performed, or sleep at the hotels where they sold out shows. **Segregation** laws still prevented Louis from enjoying the rights that white people had, even though he was becoming one of the most famous musicians of all time.

Louis's style of performing was distinctive. Up until then, bands played without any one performer standing out. Louis changed all that when he started stepping up and playing solos. Louis also switched to playing the trumpet, and he could hit high notes on the instrument that no one else could hit. He pushed the notes out so hard that he often hurt his lips, and they would bleed by the end of the night. Even though his skill was so good that he was regarded as the world's greatest trumpeter, he was also very playful in his performances. He wrote songs with titles like "Gut Bucket Blues," "Heebie Jeebies," and "Potato Head Blues." In addition to playing the trumpet, he also sang in his unmistakable rough voice. One journalist described his voice as "a wheelbarrow crunching up on a gravel driveway." He didn't try to sound proper or perfect when he sang—he just allowed his personality and flair to shine through. Audiences loved it!

> **"THAT'S ME AND I DON'T WANT TO BE NOBODY ELSE. THEY KNOW I'M THERE IN THE CAUSE OF HAPPINESS."**

In just three years, Louis recorded more than sixty records with his band, Louis Armstrong and His Hot Five. He made jazz music popular and accessible to everyone. He transformed the rhythms and sounds of jazz music in the 1920s, and influenced later musical styles from the blues to rock 'n' roll to R&B and hip-hop. He also performed about three hundred concerts a year, as well as writing books about his life and articles for newspapers and magazines. He loved to respond to letters from his fans.

Louis was married four times, but he didn't have any children of his own. He adopted his cousin's son, Clarence, when Clarence was three years old. Clarence's mother had died, and he also had a few health problems because of an injury he suffered when he was a baby. Louis raised Clarence as if he were his biological son for the rest of his life.

Louis was also an all-around entertainer. He made his first TV appearance in 1932 in a short film called *Rhapsody in Black and Blue*. He was also the first Black entertainer to appear in a major Hollywood film, in 1936, with his role in *Pennies from Heaven*. Though he didn't have any training as an actor, Louis appeared in more than a dozen films throughout his career.

Louis earned many nicknames over the years. He was known for his wide smile, and early on some fellow performers used to call him "Satchel Mouth" (a satchel is a large bag). Later, when he was performing a concert in England, someone pronounced this as "Satchmo." The new nickname stuck. When he wrote his autobiography, that's what he titled it: *Satchmo*. His friends also called him "Pops." Louis always made sure that when people did use his real name, they pronounced it with the "s" at the end and not "Louie" because, he said, he wasn't French!

Louis died of a heart attack on July 6, 1971, at age sixty-nine. Still, his music and his influence live on in his recordings, and in his impact on the music of today.

EXPLORE MORE! There are many recordings of Louis Armstrong singing and playing the trumpet. Find a few of his popular songs, like "What a Wonderful World" and "Cheek to Cheek," and see if you can sing along!

TIPS FOR YOU! Are you interested in playing music? See if your school, community, or house of worship has a band or choir you can join.

Rachel
CARSON
(1907–1964)

Rachel Carson changed how people thought about their relationship with nature. With her clear writing, she showed that using chemicals like pesticides, which are used to kill pests that are bad for plants, could actually cause more harm than good. Rachel is considered the mother of modern environmentalism.

Rachel Carson was born on May 27, 1907, in Springdale, Pennsylvania. She had an older brother and an older sister. As the youngest, she enjoyed spending time by herself, exploring the forests near her family's farm. Life was difficult for her family because they didn't have much money. Sometimes they didn't have any food for dinner, except for some apples they picked themselves. Rachel was a very good student, and her mother knew that an education would help Rachel have a better life.

Rachel graduated from high school and then received a partial scholarship to Pennsylvania College for Women. Her mother sold chickens and apples to help pay for the rest of Rachel's tuition, and even traveled to Rachel's dorm on the weekends to help Rachel type her papers. Rachel met a professor named Mary Scott Skinker who inspired her love of biology and science. When Rachel graduated from college in 1928 with top grades, she took a summer job at the Marine Biology Laboratory in Woods Hole, Massachusetts. She loved learning about the ocean and the animals in the sea.

Rachel continued her studies at Johns Hopkins University, where she focused on zoology (the study of animals). She was one of only five female students. In 1932, she received a master's degree. She enrolled as a PhD student, but had to drop out to help support her family. In the 1930s, in the middle of the Great Depression, it was difficult for people to find work. Her older siblings moved in with Rachel and their parents, so they could all help one another.

Rachel was a brilliant scientist, but she was also a very talented writer. She got a job as a scriptwriter for an educational radio show about sea life. Some of her scripts were so good that her boss submitted them to magazines. In 1937, Rachel published an essay, titled "Undersea," in the *Atlantic Monthly* magazine. The piece described in detail a journey along the ocean floor. She used the name R. L. Carson, so people would assume the writer was a man.

People loved Rachel's magazine articles about the sea and marine animals so much that they encouraged her to write a book. In 1940, she published *Under the Sea Wind,* a book about the birds, fish, and eels on the Atlantic Coast. It was written almost like poetry, but it also contained important scientific information.

In 1941, the United States entered World War II on the side of Great Britain, France, the Soviet Union, and China against Germany, Italy, and Japan. During the war, the military began using a chemical called DDT to kill bugs and pests that could spread diseases that made soldiers sick. After the war, American households started using DDT to kill bugs in their yards and homes. Farmers also started using it to kill pests on their crops. But scientists began to notice that fish were dying in the rivers, birds were dying at alarming rates, and pets were getting very sick.

Meanwhile, Rachel continued to support her family and write beautiful books about science and the ocean. In 1946, she wrote about federal wildlife preserves, and in 1951 she published a book called *The Sea Around Us* that became a best seller. It sold more than 100,000 copies. Four years later, she came out with another best seller about ocean life, called *The Edge of the Sea*. Her father had died many years earlier, and she had been supporting her mother, her two nieces, and her grandnephew. The money from the books changed Rachel's life. She finally had enough money to buy a comfortable house and take care of everyone she loved. Rachel never married, but she had a close-knit family.

Scientists and other writers adored Rachel's work. She was friends with E. B. White, the author of the popular children's book *Charlotte's Web*. They sent many letters back and forth to each other, discussing nature and **ecology**. Her scientist friends also started sending her letters about the effects they were seeing from DDT. They reported that bird species, like bald eagles and peregrine falcons, were dying out, even though DDT was only supposed to kill bugs. They knew that Rachel would be interested in their findings, and that she was so good at writing about science that she might be able to put together a book from the research.

> **"THOSE WHO DWELL AMONG THE BEAUTIES AND MYSTERIES OF THE EARTH ARE NEVER ALONE OR WEARY OF LIFE."**

At this time Rachel became very sick from cancer. She had to go to the hospital for several surgeries, and at home she wrote from her bed or from a wheelchair. She was also raising her grandnephew all by herself. Despite all the stress and illness in her life, she was determined to write a book warning about what was happening to the environment because of DDT.

In her book, Rachel pointed out that even though DDT was intended to only kill insects, birds eat those insects and also ingest the poison. She named her book *Silent Spring*, because birds that should have been chirping in the spring were found dead on the ground. She noted that when other animals eat the birds, the poison travels up the food chain, even to humans. The chemicals that farmers were spraying on their crops get into the ground, and humans consume them through food and water. She explained that if we poison nature, we poison ourselves.

When her book came out in 1962, bookstores could hardly keep it on the shelves! Everyone wanted a copy. President John F. Kennedy even mentioned it in one of his speeches. Parents everywhere wanted to read it to find out how to keep their children safe from chemicals. But the chemical companies were furious at Rachel and tried to discredit her research. Nonetheless, Rachel showed people how to understand the science and apply it in their own lives. She explained ecology so that average people could understand the concepts.

Sadly, Rachel died in 1964 from her long battle with cancer. But her message lives on in her books and writings. In 1970, Americans celebrated the first annual Earth Day. President Richard Nixon also established the Environmental Protection Agency to study and regulate the effects of humans on the environment. Because of her love for nature and through the power of her writing, Rachel Carson made the earth a safer place to live for us all.

EXPLORE MORE! Rachel loved wildlife preserves and national parks. Are there any national or state parks or preserves near you? Find out at NPS.gov or StateParks .org and see if you can visit one!

TIPS FOR YOU! When Rachel was ten years old, a children's magazine published a story she wrote! Ask an adult, like a parent, teacher, or librarian, if there are any story contests for kids that you can enter—or, see if there is a children's magazine you'd like to read.

Daniel
INOUYE
(1924–2012)

D aniel Inouye was a World War II hero and a long-serving member of the U.S. Senate. Daniel rose above racial discrimination to serve both his country and his beloved Hawaiian islands for more than half a century.

Daniel was born on September 7, 1924, and grew up on the beautiful island of Oahu in Hawaii. His grandparents, like thousands of other people from Japan, the Philippines, Portugal, and China, had come to Hawaii in the early 1900s to work on sugar plantations under unfair conditions. Since Daniel's parents were of Japanese descent, they were prevented from getting high-paying jobs, so they lived in a poor area of Honolulu. Still, they raised Daniel in a warm, loving household and taught him to spearfish, swim, and surf.

Growing up, Daniel wanted to be a surgeon, so he signed up for an American Red Cross first-aid course to work on his skills.

On the morning of December 7, 1941, seventeen-year-old Daniel was getting ready to go to church with his family after breakfast. Suddenly, they heard planes, explosions, and sirens, and saw that Japanese aircraft were bombing the naval base in Honolulu, Pearl Harbor. Daniel and his dad raced outside, shocked and furious to see the Japanese planes destroying ships and killing both soldiers and nearby civilians.

Because Daniel was a Red Cross volunteer, he rode his bike to an elementary school where they were treating injured civilians. Seventy civilians died that day, in addition to 2,400 military personnel. For five days straight, Daniel volunteered, treating injured patients. For the rest of his senior year in high school, he went to school during the day, then volunteered at the Red Cross for twelve-hour night shifts.

Immediately after the horrific attack on Pearl Harbor, the United States entered World War II on the side of the Allied Powers (Great Britain, France, the Soviet Union, and China). Daniel wanted to volunteer to fight in the war against Japan, Germany, and Italy. He was a **Nisei**, someone born in the United States to parents who immigrated from Japan. Daniel's mom had been born in the United States, but her citizenship was taken away when she married Daniel's dad, who was an immigrant. There was a law banning Asian immigrants from ever becoming citizens. Even though Daniel was a citizen, he was called an "enemy alien" by the government, and they would not allow him or other Nisei men to join the military.

In 1942, Daniel started college at the University of Hawaii. He wanted to become a doctor. However, after a petition from Nisei men, the U.S. government changed its policy and allowed men of Japanese descent to join the war effort. In 1943, Daniel, like 85 percent of the other Nisei men in Hawaii, joined the 442nd Regimental Combat Team, an all–Japanese American unit. He trained for ten months in Camp Shelby, Mississippi.

One day, his unit visited an internment camp in nearby Arkansas, where Japanese Americans were imprisoned behind barbed-wire fences. All over the United States, Japanese Americans had been forced to leave their homes, businesses, and belongings, to be held in camps where they were monitored by guards. The government unfairly thought they might be spies for the Japanese army, even though most Nisei, like Daniel, had never been to Japan.

Daniel and his combat team shipped out to Italy to fight against the German army, the Nazis. The 442nd Regiment's motto was "Go for Broke!" which means to give everything you have in battle. In eastern France, they fought the German army in hand-to-hand combat to liberate a French town that had been taken over by the Nazis. Daniel was awarded the rank of second lieutenant for his leadership and bravery. On April 21, 1945, he was fighting in a battle in Italy when he was shot in the side by a German soldier. The enemy fire nearly tore off his right arm, which he later lost due to the injury. Nonetheless, he was able to throw a grenade into an enemy bunker. Daniel was awarded a Distinguished Service Cross, a Bronze Star medal, and a Purple Heart medal. The 442nd

Regiment lost many men in World War II, but they are the most decorated unit of their size in the entire history of the U.S. military.

Daniel spent nearly two years recovering from his injuries in a military hospital. After the war's end, he returned home to Hawaii. On the way, during a stop in California, he tried to get a haircut but the shop owner called him a racial slur and refused to serve him. Even in his army uniform and missing an arm that he sacrificed for America's freedom, he was still treated as a second-class citizen. He wanted to make a change.

> **"WE WANTED TO TAKE OUR FULL PLACE IN SOCIETY, TO MAKE THE GREATEST CONTRIBUTION OF WHICH WE WERE CAPABLE."**

Since his dreams of being a surgeon had been shattered when he lost his arm, Daniel went back to college to pursue law as a career. In college, he met Margaret Awamura and proposed to her on their second date. (She said yes.) After attending law school at George Washington University in Washington, DC, Daniel wanted to use his knowledge and expertise in politics. In 1954, he won a seat in the U.S. House of Representatives.

When Daniel first became a congressman, Hawaii was not yet a state. It was a U.S. territory (like Puerto Rico and Guam). Hawaii became the fiftieth state in 1959.

Many residents of Hawaii were excited to have better representation in government. But many Indigenous Hawaiians still mourned the loss of the nation that they had ruled for hundreds of years before the United States took over.

When Hawaii became a state, its people also gained the right to have two U.S. senators. In the U.S. government, there are two houses of Congress—the House of Representatives and the Senate. When Daniel Inouye was elected to the Senate in 1962, he became the first Japanese American elected to Congress. Daniel served the people of Hawaii as their senator for forty years.

During his time in office, Daniel was known for his wisdom, his calm manner, and his willingness to work with others. He secured funding for education and housing in Hawaii, and also helped pass a bill that officially apologized to the Japanese Americans who were held in the internment camps during World War II. They each received **reparations**, or a payment, of $20,000. Many Japanese Americans in Southern California donated their payment to build a museum in Los Angeles's Little Tokyo, called the Japanese American National Museum.

President Bill Clinton presented Daniel with the Medal of Honor, the nation's highest military decoration, in 2000. When Daniel Inouye died in 2012, President Barack Obama, who was also born in Hawaii, spoke at his funeral, saying that Daniel Inouye had been his first political inspiration.

EXPLORE MORE! Check out GoForBroke.org to hear more stories from men from the 442nd Regimental Combat unit. Or, if you're ever in Los Angeles, visit the Go For Broke National Education Center Exhibition and Monument.

TIPS FOR YOU! You may have family members or family friends who also served in the military, like Daniel Inouye. Find out if they are willing to tell you any stories about their experience.

César
CHÁVEZ
(1927–1993)

Césario "César" Estrada Chávez had a deep understanding of the challenges faced by farmworkers. César dedicated his life to improving the working conditions of the workers who brought fresh food to people's tables, even though the workers themselves often went hungry.

Césario was born on March 31, 1927, near Yuma, Arizona. His parents owned a farm where they grew cotton, watermelon, and alfalfa. His mother, Juana, believed strongly in taking care of those who were less fortunate, and she would send her kids out to find men without housing and invite them to dinner at the Chávez home. But in 1938, the family lost their farm due to unpaid property taxes. When Césario was twelve, his family moved to Oxnard in central California to find work on farms there.

At school, Césario's teachers called him "César" and forbid him from speaking any Spanish. The other kids made fun of César for wearing the same clothes every day, even though his older sister washed them every night.

César and his family sometimes lived in other people's garages, since they moved around so often to find work in the fields. In the winter they planted onions, in the spring they harvested carrots and broccoli, in the early summer they picked plums, and in the late summer they moved on to peach and tomato farms. Everyone in his family worked. It was very difficult to stoop over for hours in the hot sun every day, planting and harvesting.

When César was a teenager, his family moved to Delano, California. In 1946, he enlisted in the U.S. Navy and served in Guam. When he returned home from the Navy, he married a girl he knew from Delano named Helen, and they had eight children.

César didn't receive a high school diploma, because he always worked in the fields when he was a teenager. After he and Helen got married, he worked in a lumber-yard. During this time, César met a priest named Father Donald McDonnell, who was Irish Catholic and spoke Spanish. The priest was an activist who worked in the Mexican American community. He conducted Mass on Sunday nights and weekday evenings, so the farmwork-ers could attend church without having to miss any work. César also teamed up with an activist named Fred Ross. Together, he and Fred opened chapters of the Community Service Organization (CSO), a Latinx civil rights organi-zation founded by Fred.

César met Fred Ross and Father Donald McDonnell when he was twenty-six and immediately started volunteering to help his community. He stacked lumber during the day, and at night and on weekends he helped Mexican Americans register to vote, giving them materials printed in Spanish and helping them follow the voter-registration procedures. César also came up with fund-raising ideas, like Christmas tree sales and children's fairs, to raise money for the CSO. Because of his work in the community, he spent a lot of time away from his family, but he had learned that his passion in life was to help other Mexican Americans get ahead.

In the 1950s, many of the half million farmworkers were people of Mexican descent. This was because in the 1940s the United States brought in many people from Mexico to fill the jobs that were left open by Americans going to fight in World War II. These farmworkers were not protected by labor laws the way most employees were. Sometimes they were not paid what they were promised or had no bathrooms to use and not enough water to drink in the fields. If workers were treated disrespectfully or abused by their employers, there was nothing they could do.

César had learned how to organize and bring communities together from his work with the CSO. He was passionate, determined, and skilled, and worked to organize a farmworkers' union.

"IT IS HOW WE USE OUR LIVES THAT DETERMINES WHAT KIND OF MEN WE ARE."

Through his friend Fred Ross at the CSO, César met a fellow organizer named Dolores Huerta. Dolores wanted to be a teacher, but when she saw how many of her Mexican American students were coming to school hungry and with no shoes, she decided she needed to help them directly. In the spring of 1962, Dolores and César founded an organization that later became the United Farm Workers (UFW). Its mission was to improve wages and working conditions for farmworkers in the United States. *Dolores* means "pain" in Spanish and *Huerta* means "orchard," so César joked that she was destined to work to alleviate pain in the orchards.

César, Dolores, and their many fellow organizers started a newspaper in 1964 to spread information about strikes and boycotts. César organized a peaceful three-hundred-mile march from Delano to the state capital, Sacramento, to speak with politicians and draw attention to their cause with signs and chants. César walked with a cane because he had blisters on his feet from walking so far.

Meanwhile, many Filipino American farmworkers had realized that one effective strategy to get better pay and working conditions was to **strike**, or refuse to work. In grape vineyards, for example, it was important to harvest the grapes quickly and put them into storage. An activist named Larry Itliong led his fellow Filipino American workers in a strike to protest a pay cut. If the grape growers could not get their produce harvested, they were more likely to listen to the demands of the workers because they would risk losing money. César and the Mexican American farmworkers agreed to strike, too.

People heard about the strike and came to Delano to volunteer and offer support. Although the UFW was mostly made up of Mexican American workers, people of all backgrounds came to support César, especially fellow Catholics. César's greatest honor was being invited to Rome to meet the pope, the leader of the Catholic church. The pope sent gifts home with César and Helen to give to their children.

César believed in sacrifice and suffering, so he often fasted, or refused to eat. He was a vegetarian and only ate organic foods. Although he fought to make sure that farmworkers could make a living wage, he did not ask to be paid much money for his work. He believed that too much money corrupted people.

César died in 1993. Thousands of people attended his funeral in Delano, marching in a three-mile procession, similar to one of the marches that he led. Today, people in California, Colorado, and Texas celebrate César Chávez Day on his birthday, March 31. In 1994, his family accepted the Presidential Medal of Freedom in his honor, presented by President Bill Clinton. César will always be remembered for fighting to make sure that the people who grow our food can also feed their own families.

EXPLORE MORE! Look up a painting called *Sun Mad* by Ester Hernandez and think about the artist's message about agricultural work.

TIPS FOR YOU! Farmers' markets are great places to find delicious locally grown food, support farmers in your community, and learn more about farming practices. Find out if there are any near you!

Martin Luther
KING JR.
(1929–1968)

Martin Luther King Jr., an American preacher and civil rights activist, was born in Atlanta, Georgia, on January 15, 1929. Martin was a very good student and skipped two grades in high school. He entered Morehouse College at the age of fifteen. After graduation, Martin decided to become a minister and attended Crozer Theological Seminary in Pennsylvania. Afterward, in 1951, he enrolled at Boston University, where he received a doctorate degree in theology. Martin was just twenty-five years old.

While Martin was studying in Boston, he met a talented young musician named Coretta Scott. She was working on her degree in voice and violin at the New England Conservatory of Music. Coretta was also an activist. The two started dating, and they were married in 1953. They had four children.

After their wedding, Martin and Coretta moved to Montgomery, Alabama, where Martin became the pastor of a church. During this time—the early 1950s—many

Black people in Montgomery rode the bus to get to work and to run errands. But the law said that they had to move to the back of any bus if a white person boarded and wanted to take their seat. A group called the National Association for the Advancement of Colored People (NAACP) was fighting back against this unfair law, and many others.

On December 1, 1955, a woman named Rosa Parks refused to give up her seat for a white passenger and was arrested. Martin joined forces with the NAACP, and they took up Rosa's cause. Martin organized the Black residents of Montgomery to refuse to ride the buses until the unfair laws were changed. When you refuse to support a company because it has unfair practices, that is called a boycott.

Word spread quickly. The Black riders found other ways to get around Montgomery, and the boycott continued for weeks, then for months. Soon after it began, the activists filed a lawsuit to end segregation on the buses. The case made it all the way to the **U.S. Supreme Court**, which declared that the laws discriminating against Black people on the buses were unconstitutional. Finally, after 382 days—more than a year!—the Montgomery bus boycott brought an end to bus segregation.

Martin became well known as a result of the bus boycott. He was just twenty-six years old, but he was an inspiring leader. He showed people what could be accomplished through nonviolent protest. Despite his own commitment to nonviolence, some Montgomery residents who did not want Black people to have equal rights threw bombs through his window and shot a bullet through his front door. Still, he remained dedicated to fighting inequality.

In 1963, the leaders of the major civil rights groups came together to organize a march in the nation's capital to make a big statement about how Black people were discriminated against. The event was called the March on Washington for Jobs and Freedom, and on August 28, 1963, more than 250,000 people came together in Washington, DC. Reporters and television stations covered the event as prominent leaders, including Martin, gave speeches. As he stood in the shadow of the Lincoln Memorial, Martin spoke of the joyous day a century earlier when Abraham Lincoln signed the Emancipation Proclamation. "But one hundred years later, the Negro is still not free," he declared. Black people still lived in a country with segregation and were not allowed to do the things white people could do or be in the places where white people could be. Many white Americans during this time had more money and possessions than they ever had before. But for Black people, Martin said, living in America was like living on "a lonely island of poverty" in the middle of an ocean full of people with money.

Martin used his speech to remind everyone not to be overcome by hate and not to use violence in pursuit of justice. He acknowledged the white Americans in the crowd who were fighting for freedom for all. He condemned police brutality and businesses that refused to serve Black Americans. He spoke out against laws preventing Black people from exercising their right to vote. Martin told the crowd, despite all the promises to Black people that had been broken, he still had a dream.

> **"I HAVE A DREAM THAT ONE DAY THIS NATION WILL RISE UP, LIVE OUT THE TRUE MEANING OF ITS CREED: 'WE HOLD THESE TRUTHS TO BE SELF-EVIDENT, THAT ALL MEN ARE CREATED EQUAL.'"**

Although Martin spent many years fighting for civil rights in the U.S., he was also concerned about freedom and peace all over the world. During the 1960s, the U.S. was involved in a war in Vietnam, a country in Southeast Asia. Many American soldiers were dying in this war, as well as Vietnamese civilians (people who were not soldiers). Martin believed it was wrong to kill Vietnamese people and destroy their land, especially when there was social welfare work to be done at home.

Martin also believed that poverty was one of the most important problems to address as he worked for equality. He recognized that people could not truly be free or equal when they couldn't afford basic necessities, like food and housing. He called this goal **economic justice**. Martin fought to make sure that Black people had equal access to the jobs and resources that would allow them to be economically secure. He also recognized that poverty affected many groups of people. In Atlanta, he met with a group that included Black people, Indigenous People, Latinx people, and white people from rural areas like the Appalachian Mountains.

Martin won the Nobel Peace Prize in 1964, when he was only thirty-five years old—the youngest person ever to receive the award. Only people who have truly made the world a safer and more harmonious place are awarded this prize.

On April 4, 1968, Martin was assassinated in Memphis, Tennessee. He was there to give a speech calling for better wages and working conditions for the local garbage workers. While he was standing on the balcony of his hotel room, a man named James Earl Ray shot and killed him. Today, we celebrate Martin in January every year. During his lifetime, he was jailed, harassed, and beaten as he fought for civil rights. He dedicated his life to the pursuit of peace and freedom.

EXPLORE MORE! Listen to Martin's "I Have a Dream" speech, compare it with his original written draft, and explore animations at FreedomsRing.Stanford.edu.

TIPS FOR YOU! Martin Luther King Jr. led many marches in order to bring about the changes he wanted to see in his country. Find out if there are any marches or events in your community that raise awareness about causes that you care about, and talk to your parent or caregiver about whether you can join one.

Sandra Day
O'CONNOR
(1930–)

Sandra Day O'Connor made history when she became the first woman appointed to the U.S. Supreme Court. Court observers thought that she would be another conservative voice. Over time, however, people saw that she had an independent streak. Her sensible approach guided her thinking, and she often provided the crucial deciding vote in some of the most controversial issues that came before the Court.

Sandra was born on March 26, 1930, to Ada Mae and Harry Day. The Days lived on a large cattle ranch in Arizona that they called the Lazy B Ranch. Her parents could see that Sandra was very smart, but good schools were far from their ranch. They decided to send her to school in El Paso, where she lived with her grandparents.

After elementary school, Sandra attended a boarding school for girls. Sandra's friends said she had a "cowgirl accent," and, at school, students had to learn to speak properly.

Sandra skipped two grades, graduated from high school at age sixteen, and went to Stanford University in California. She excelled in college, and she decided to continue at Stanford and go to law school to become an attorney. In law school she met a fellow student, from San Francisco, named John O'Connor. They dated for a little while and then got married at the Lazy B Ranch in 1952.

Everything seemed to be going perfectly for Sandra. She graduated in the top 10 percent of her law school class. Then, she passed a very difficult test that lawyers have to take, called the **bar exam**. But when she applied for more than forty jobs, no law firms would hire her. They said they had never hired a woman before. One firm offered her a typing job instead. Sandra really wanted to do the job that she had worked so hard to become qualified for, so she ended up working for a district attorney for no pay and without a desk.

After living in Germany during the 1950s, while John O'Connor served in the military, the O'Connors moved back to the United States and settled in Phoenix, Arizona. John got a job at a law firm, but still no law firms wanted to hire a woman. Sandra decided to open her own small law practice with another lawyer in a shopping mall. During this time she had three sons.

Though law firms still refused to hire her, in 1965 Sandra found a job working for the government as the state assistant attorney general of Arizona. The attorney general is the main legal adviser for the government. Sandra loved her job, and she was good at what she did. Working for the government also gave her an opportunity to get involved in politics. In 1969, she became the first woman ever appointed to the Arizona State Senate. She was elected on her own the following year, and in 1973 she became the majority leader, which meant that she was the highest-ranking person in the legislature.

During the 1970s, it was still rare for women to hold political office. However, many women became active in women's rights issues, and they tried to get politicians to change sexist laws. Sandra was in office during a time when women were fighting for more political power and legal rights. This activism affected her decisions as a lawyer and a politician. She was dedicated to reforming laws that discriminated against women.

Sandra thought she could do even more good as a judge, so she decided to run for state court judge. Her three boys helped her campaign in her community, and she ended up getting elected to the court in 1975. Sandra was a tough judge, and lawyers knew they had to come to her court-room prepared. She also went out of her way to mentor young women in the legal field. She wanted to help more women break into the profession, as she had.

In 1979, she was promoted to the Arizona Court of Appeals. Two years later, there was an open position on the U.S. Supreme Court, the highest court in the entire country.

In 1981, President Reagan appointed Sandra Day O'Connor to the U.S. Supreme Court, and her nomination was unanimously approved by the Senate. Sandra became the first woman to ever hold that position. Twenty-five years earlier, no law firm would hire her; now she was one of the nine most powerful justices in the country.

Sandra served on the Court with eight other justices, and she also hired people to work on her staff. Judges hire **clerks**—lawyers who help by doing research and writing the opinions about the cases that come before the court. Sandra always made sure that half her clerks were women. She also hired clerks who held different views than hers and had a different background than she did. She knew that this policy would create a stronger team. Sandra also started an aerobics class for people working at or near the court to get some exercise. They even had matching T-shirts!

> **"I HOPE I HAVE HELPED PAVE THE PATHWAY FOR OTHER WOMEN WHO HAVE CHOSEN TO FOLLOW A CAREER. OUR PURPOSE IN LIFE IS TO HELP OTHERS ALONG THE WAY."**

When Sandra was fifty-eight, she received unexpected news. Though she was very healthy and active, she was diagnosed with cancer. She was devastated. She had to have surgery and take medicine that made her hair fall out. Still, she continued to work on the Supreme Court. She wore a wig and rested on the weekends.

During her twenty-four-year career on the Supreme Court, Sandra was known for thoughtful and deliberate decisions. She took cases regarding children very seriously, and ruled in a case that allowed children to testify in court by video. She did not believe that it was fair to make children sit in the same room with someone who had hurt them.

In 2006, Sandra stepped down from the Supreme Court. Her husband had developed Alzheimer's, a disease that affected his brain and his memory. She wanted to be able to spend more time with him. Through her career as a justice, Sandra made an undeniable impact on history. In 2009, President Barack Obama recognized her with the Presidential Medal of Freedom. The law school at Arizona State University was renamed the Sandra Day O'Connor College of Law. She also helped create a website with video games that teach students about civics and government.

EXPLORE MORE! Check out Sandra Day O'Connor's amazing website, iCivics.org! The games are super fun, and you can practice being a lawyer or a judge, or even being president!

TIPS FOR YOU! Sandra Day O'Connor was the first female U.S. Supreme Court justice. What do professionals look like in the career that you want to have? Remember, even if most of them don't look like you, you can still do any job you want to!

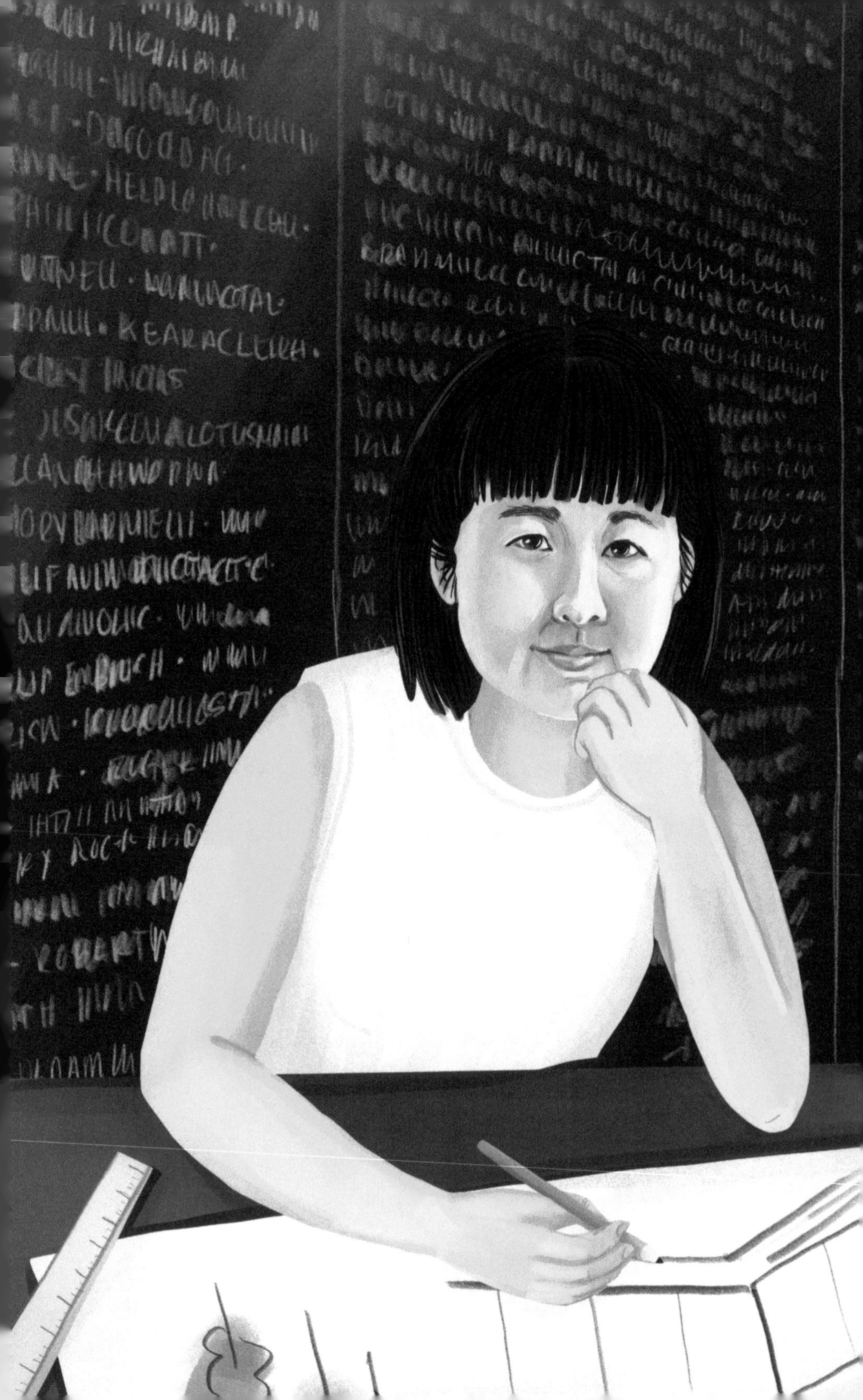

Maya
LIN
(1959–)

Maya Ying Lin is one of America's most influential and groundbreaking artists. She was propelled into the public spotlight at the age of twenty-one when she proposed a controversial idea for the Vietnam Veterans Memorial in Washington, DC. She has designed numerous memorials as well as public and private buildings. She draws her inspiration from nature.

Maya was born on October 5, 1959, in Athens, Ohio. Her parents had escaped from China in the 1940s during a brutal civil war there. Maya's parents had experienced **censorship** in China, meaning the government does not allow you to read, write, or say certain things. After escaping from Shanghai, Maya's mother went to college in the United States, earned a PhD degree, and became a professor of poetry. Maya's father was an artist who worked with ceramics. Both her parents taught at Ohio University, and they had extraordinary talents for communicating through art. Maya and her older brother, Tan, grew up in a very creative household, where their parents encouraged them to express themselves through art. Maya continued this family tradition in her work.

Maya was quiet as a young girl. There were very few other Chinese American kids in her school, and she often felt like an outcast. She got straight A's and loved to study art and math. She even took some classes at Ohio University while she was still in high school. After graduating, Maya majored in architecture at Yale University, one of the top schools in the country. Though it might seem like math and art are opposite interests, they combine perfectly in architecture, which is designing and constructing buildings.

In her senior year at Yale, Maya and her classmates and professor were inspired by a design competition for a new memorial in Washington, DC, for Vietnam War veterans. Their assignment was to incorporate the names of the 57,000 Americans who were killed or went missing during the nineteen-year conflict in Southeast Asia. Many war memorials feature images of soldiers, flags, or weapons. But Maya wanted to make a different statement. She wanted people to feel a sense of loss and sorrow. Her design included a black, V-shaped wall that cut into the earth. It would be made of reflective granite, and every fallen soldier's name would be etched into the stone. If you stood in front of the wall, you would see your own face reflected back at you as you touched the names carved into the black granite. She submitted her project to her professor and got a B+ on the assignment.

Maya also submitted her design to the contest, along with 1,420 other people, including her professor. There were no names included on any of the submissions. When her design beat out all the rest, the judges were surprised to learn that they had chosen a twenty-year-old college student as the winner of the contest! Her design was an intimate and honest way to capture the reality of the war and to remember those who died. However, the design faced immediate criticism. Some people said it looked too feminine. Some people said it looked like a black scar on the earth. Other people objected to hiring a woman of Asian descent to design a memorial for a war in Asia—even though Maya was born in Ohio and is American. Looking back on the criticism today, Maya says that good art is supposed to be controversial and spark strong reactions from people.

Maya successfully defended her innovative design before Congress and in the press. On November 13, 1982, the Vietnam Veterans Memorial was unveiled in Washington, DC. Approximately three million people visit the memorial each year, and most cannot resist reaching out to touch the names of the fallen soldiers. Many Vietnam veterans, as well as friends and family members of the soldiers, are overcome with emotion at the sight of the sheer number of names on the wall, and at the specific names of their loved ones. The memorial is both national and personal, all at once. Maya had created a world-famous sculpture before most people even begin their careers.

In the years that followed, Maya turned down most offers to design more memorials. But when she was twenty-nine the Southern Poverty Law Center asked her to design a national civil rights memorial in Montgomery, Alabama. Even though she hadn't learned much about the civil rights movement in school, Maya started reading about Martin Luther King Jr. (see page 95) and his work for social justice. She loved the line in his "I Have a Dream Speech" that says, "[We] will not be satisfied until justice rolls down like waters and righteousness like a mighty stream." She decided to incorporate water into her design.

The Civil Rights Memorial was unveiled on November 5, 1989. The granite structure is inscribed with the names of forty-one important people and dates of significant events in civil rights history. Maya wanted the memorial to teach people the history that she never learned in school. Water flows evenly and smoothly over the surface, but if you touch the water, you see the ripples you have created. The memorial symbolizes the ripple effect that just one person can have on the future.

Whereas these two impressive memorials are made out of stone, Maya also wanted to make sculptures out of other materials. In 1995, she created a sculpture for a new aerospace engineering building at the University of Michigan. This installation, called *Wave Field*, is made of waves of sandy soil that stand from three to six feet tall. You can walk among the waves, or even curl up against a wave and read a book. Some people say they actually feel seasick among the waves!

In 2004, Maya had the opportunity to design a museum that incorporated her own family history. For the Museum of Chinese in America, located in Manhattan, New York, she drew on the architecture of her father's childhood home in Fujian Province in China. She highlighted the history of the 1882 Chinese Exclusion Act, which banned Chinese people from immigrating to the United States because of their race. She also devoted an area to Angel Island, in San Francisco Bay, California, where Chinese immigrants were detained for questioning and health screenings, sometimes for months. Maya's goal for the museum was that each visitor would feel as if they were having a private conversation with the exhibits within a public space.

Maya also used her creativity to teach people about the effects that the famous American explorers Lewis and Clark had on the physical environment. The year 2005 marked the two-hundred-year anniversary of Lewis and Clark's expedition into the newly acquired western portion of the United States. In what is now called the Pacific Northwest, the explorers encountered the Nez Perce, Umatilla, and Chinook peoples. Maya worked closely with the tribes to build six different interactive stations along the Columbia River. The landscape installations are called the Confluence Project. They highlight the changes in plants, animals, and people in the last two hundred years. The project incorporates Chinook myths and blessings, preserving them in the earth and rock.

Today Maya is passionate about using her talents to highlight endangered species and to help people pay closer attention to nature. She creates interactive sculptures and spaces in museums all over the country. In 2016, she received the Presidential Medal of Freedom from Barack Obama for her extraordinary memorials and sculptures. She married Daniel Wolf in 1996, and they have two daughters. Maya Lin has forever changed the way we honor our past, and her works inspire us to build a brighter future.

EXPLORE MORE! Go to Maya Lin's website, WhatIsMissing.net, to learn more about endangered species and habitats, and what you can do to help. Use what you learn to try making a plan for how you and your family can help the environment.

TIPS FOR YOU! Maya Lin uses sculptures, architecture, art installations, and memorials to express what she cares about. Try building a small sculpture, based on a cause you care about. You can start with craft materials or even recycled things from your home—just be sure to ask an adult first whether you can use them.

More Inspiring People to Explore

Phillis Wheatley
Early American poet
1753–1784

Kidnapped from her home in West Africa as a child, Phillis Wheatley learned to read and write in New England and became an internationally recognized poet and writer.

Alexander Hamilton
Founding father of the United States
1755 or 1757–1804

Alexander Hamilton, one of the founding fathers of the United States, established our financial system.

William Lloyd Garrison
Abolitionist, journalist, and social reformer
1805–1879

William Lloyd Garrison started an apprenticeship at a newspaper at age thirteen, and then established his own newspaper, called The Liberator, to connect the community of abolitionists.

Hiram R. Revels
First Black U.S. senator
1827–1901

Hiram Revels, the first Black U.S. senator, represented the state of Mississippi right after the Civil War.

W. E. B. Du Bois
Sociologist and founder of the NAACP
1868–1963

William Edward Burghardt Du Bois, the first Black man to earn a PhD from Harvard, wrote dozens of acclaimed essays, novels, and books about the Black experience in America.

Hattie Wyatt Caraway
First woman elected to the U.S. Senate
1878–1950

Hattie Wyatt Caraway was the first woman to run for and win a Senate race (in 1932). She represented the state of Arkansas.

Zitkála-Šá
Indigenous People rights advocate
1876–1938
A member of the Dakota tribe, Zitkála-Šá wrote several books, fought for the rights of Indigenous Peoples to become American citizens, and was the first Indigenous American to write an opera.

Eleanor Roosevelt
First Lady and delegate to the United Nations
1884–1962
The thirty-fourth First Lady of the United States, Eleanor Roosevelt advocated for the rights of women, Black people, and Asian Americans, and was the first U.S. delegate to the United Nations Commission on Human Rights.

Dalip Singh Saund
First Asian American elected to the U.S. House of Representatives
1899–1973
Born in Chhajulwadi, India, Dalip Singh Saund immigrated to the United States to study mathematics at UC Berkeley and became the first Asian American, Indian American, and Sikh American to be elected to the House of Representatives. He represented the state of California.

Fred Korematsu
Civil rights activist
1919–2005

In 1942, during World War II, Fred Korematsu refused to go to an internment camp simply because he was a Japanese American, sparking a civil rights battle that went all the way to the U.S. Supreme Court.

James Baldwin
Poet, playwright, and novelist
1924–1987

James Baldwin believed that segregation and racism hurt both Black and white communities, and he wrote about his beliefs in beautiful essays and novels, including Notes of a Native Son.

Althea Gibson
Professional golfer and tennis player
1927–2003

Althea Gibson was the first Black woman to win the Grand Slam title in tennis (in 1956), and the first Black woman to compete on the Women's Professional Golf Tour in the 1960s.

Harvey Milk
First openly gay elected official in California
1930–1978

During his short time on the San Francisco Board of Supervisors, Harvey Milk fought discrimination against people based on their sexual orientation. Sadly, he was assassinated just eleven months into his historic term as the first openly gay man to hold public office in California.

Judith Heumann
Disability rights activist
1947–

Judith Heumann, a lifelong advocate for the disability community, led a twenty-eight-day sit-in at the Department of Health, Education, and Welfare to help pass legislation that guarantees rights for people with disabilities.

Sonia Sotomayor
First Latinx U.S. Supreme Court justice
1954–

Born in the Bronx, New York, Sonia Sotomayor attended Princeton and Yale before becoming a lawyer and then being appointed the first Latinx Supreme Court justice in U.S. history.

Glossary

abolish: to officially end a law, custom, or institution

abolitionists: people who believe that slavery should be illegal

architecture: designing and constructing buildings

Articles of Confederation: the first government of the United States

assimilating: changing your way of life to be more like the people around you

autobiography: the story of a person's life as written by that person

bar exam: a test you have to take to become a lawyer

boycott: to refuse to buy from a company you don't agree with

censorship: when the government does not allow you to read, write, or say certain things

census: a count of all the people in an area

checks and balances: a political system which stops any one person from having too much power

civilians: people who are not soldiers

clerk: someone who assists a judge with research and writing legal opinions

ecology: the relation of plants and organisms to each other and their environment

economic justice: the idea that the economy will be more successful if it is fairer

Fugitive Slave Law: a law that allowed law enforcement officers to kidnap former slaves in the North and bring them back to the South

Great Depression: the worst economic downturn in U.S. history (1929–1933)

Harlem Renaissance: an artistic, social, and intellectual movement in the Black community of New York in the 1920s

impeach: to put a political figure on trial for bad behavior or a crime

internment camps: camps established during World War II to isolate Japanese Americans

Jim Crow laws: laws that separated white and Black people, after the Civil War, discriminating against Black people

land surveyor: a person who explores lands that have not been mapped yet

lynching: when unofficial juries try, convict, and put to death someone without going through the legal system

memoirs: someone's life stories

military strategy: the art of coming up with a plan for an army in battle or war

Morse code: a method of communication using dots and dashes to represent letters through a tapping device

New Deal: a series of government programs and public works projects, put in place between 1933 and 1939, to help stimulate the U.S. economy and get Americans back to work during and after the Great Depression

Nisei: someone born in the United States to Japanese immigrant parents

overseer: a person who worked on a plantation to enforce rules that enslaved people had to follow

pacifist: someone who does not believe in war

polio: a contagious virus that is disabling and life-threatening

ratified: agreed upon by enough states to pass a law to enact the Constitution or amend it

Reconstruction: the period spanning 1865 to 1877, after the Civil War, when the North and South became unified again

renegotiate: to discuss an agreement again, usually in order to change it

reparations: payment as an apology for something done wrong

secede: to break away from

segregation: when different races have separate facilities and opportunities

strike: refusing to work until worker demands are met

suffrage: voting rights

unanimously: with everyone's agreement

Underground Railroad: a network of antislavery activists that helped enslaved people get to the North

U.S. Supreme Court: the highest court in the United States

Resources

Want to learn more about important people in American history? Here are some good places to start!

Books

Alexander Hamilton: The Graphic History of an American Founding Father, by Jonathan Hennessey, illustrated by Justin Greenwood

American Trailblazers, by Lisa Truisani

Asian Americans Who Inspire Us, by Analiza Quirez Wolf, with Michael Franco

Black Heroes: A Black History Book for Kids, by Arlisha Norwood

Black Women in Science, by Kimberly Brown Pellum

50 Fearless Women Who Made American History, by Jenifer Bazzit

History Smashers Series, by Kate Messner

Home of the Brave: An American History Book for Kids, by Brooke Khan

Little Leaders: Bold Women in Black History, by Vashti Harrison

Modern Herstory: Stories of Women and Nonbinary People Rewriting History, by Blair Imani

Websites

MountVernon.org: Learn more about George Washington, the Revolutionary War, and the Constitution on this amazing website!

Newsela.com: Read about current events and historical figures at the reading level of your choice.

Media

AllThePresidentsMan.Podbean.com: This podcast has an episode about every president in U.S. history!

The Who Was? Show: This Netflix show is a fun and entertaining way to learn more about historical figures.

Historical Sites and Museums

Honolulu, Hawaii: Pearl Harbor National Memorial

Los Angeles, California: Japanese American National Museum

Montgomery, Alabama: Civil Rights Memorial

New York, New York: Museum of Chinese in America

Washington, DC: National Museum of African American History and Culture

Washington, DC: National Museum of the American Indian

References

George Washington (1732–1799)

Calloway, Colin G. *The Indian World of George Washington.* Oxford, UK: Oxford University Press, 2019.

Holton, Woody. *Unruly Americans and the Origins of the Constitution.* New York: Hill and Wang, 2007.

Tecumseh (1768–1813)

Dunbar-Ortiz, Roxanne. *An Indigenous Peoples' History of the United States.* Boston: Beacon Press, 2014.

Laxer, James. *Tecumseh & Brock: The War of 1812.* Toronto: Anansi, 2012.

Lucretia Mott (1793–1880)

Faulkner, Carol. *Lucretia Mott's Heresy: Abolition and Women's Rights in Nineteenth-Century America.* Philadelphia: University of Pennsylvania Press, 2011.

Ulysses S. Grant (1822–1885)

Chernow, Ron. *Grant.* New York: Penguin Books, 2017.

Harriet Tubman (1822–1913)

Dunbar, Erica Armstrong. *She Came to Slay: The Life and Times of Harriet Tubman.* New York: Simon & Schuster, 2019.

Thomas Edison (1847–1931)

Morris, Edmund. *Edison.* New York: Random House, 2019.

Ida B. Wells (1862–1931)

Chambers, Veronica. *Finish the Fight: The Brave and Revolutionary Women Who Fought for the Right to Vote.* New York: The New York Times Company, 2020.

Giddings, Paula J. *Ida: A Sword among Lions.* New York: HarperCollins, 2009.

Dorothea Lange (1895–1965)

Gordon, Linda. *Dorothea Lange: A Life Beyond Limits.* New York: W. W. Norton & Company, 2009.

Louis Armstrong (1901–1971)

Imani, Blair. *Making Our Way Home: The Great Migration and the Black American Dream.* New York: Ten Speed Press, 2020.

Teachout, Terry. *Pops: A Life of Louis Armstrong.* New York: Mariner Books, 2009.

Rachel Carson (1907–1964)

Barnet, Andrea. *Visionary Women: How Rachel Carson, Jane Jacobs, Jane Goodall, and Alice Waters Changed Our World.* New York: HarperCollins, 2018.

Daniel Inouye (1924–2012)

Slavicek, Louise Chipley. *Daniel Inouye*. New York: Chelsea House, 2007.

César Chávez (1927–1993)

Pawel, Miriam. *The Crusades of César Chávez*. New York: Bloomsbury Press, 2014.

Martin Luther King Jr. (1929–1968)

Harding, Vincent. *Martin Luther King: The Inconvenient Hero*. Maryknoll, New York: Orbis Books, 1996.

Sandra Day O'Connor (1930–)

Thomas, Evan. *First: Sandra Day O'Connor*. New York: Random House, 2019.

Maya Lin (1959–)

Rubin, Susan Goldman. *Maya Lin: Thinking with Her Hands*. San Francisco: Chronicle Books, 2017.

Index

About the Author

Megan DuVarney Forbes is a historian and middle school teacher in Southern California. She received her master's degree in U.S. history from California State University, Fullerton. She specializes in Caribbean and civil rights history, and frequently teaches about social justice through history and literature. She enjoys spending time with her husband and son, and creating history content for teachers on her blog, TooCoolForMiddleSchool.com. You can find out more about what she is reading, teaching, and learning on her YouTube channel, Too Cool for Middle School. Megan is currently enjoying her ninth year of teaching history and English.

Author Acknowledgments

Writing this book during a pandemic with a toddler in a small apartment was a team effort. I am forever grateful to my husband, Derrick, for supporting me in my research and writing. I am also grateful to my son, Jenson, for forcing me to take breaks to play hide-and-seek!

About the Illustrator

Amanda Lenz is an illustrator and designer residing in Boulder, Colorado. The love of the outdoors, people, places, and adventure shines through her illustrative work. Ten years in a solo design and illustration practice (LenzIllustration.com) has borne a variety of rich visual work. A fine art and figure drawing practice paired with a design and digital sensibility has created a rich, colorful, and crafted illustration style. She loves telling visual stories of inspiring people, and the places and ideas they have shaped. Amanda spends her spare time sketching, gardening, and hiking with her partner and two adorable, slightly rotten dogs.

Illustrator Acknowledgments

Thank you to my beautiful family and encouraging group of friends for the support, humor, and light over this past year and beyond.

CPSIA information can be obtained
at www.ICGtesting.com
Printed in the USA
JSHW020418100621
15742JS00006B/6